BEFORE

THE

RING

Discovery House Publishers

Books, music, and videos that feed the soul with the Word of God

Box 3566 Grand Rapids, MI 49501

QUESTIONS WORTH ASKING

BEFORE

THE

RING

WILLIAM L. COLEMAN

ILLUSTRATIONS BY RON WHEELER

Before the Ring
Copyright © 1991 by William L. Coleman

Revised and expanded edition copyright © 1998
by William L. Coleman

Discovery House Publishers is affiliated with RBC Ministries, Grand
Rapids, Michigan 49512.

Unless otherwise indicated, all Scripture quotations are taken from the *Holy
Bible, New International Version.* Copyright © 1973, 1978, 1984 by
International Bible Society. Used by permission of Zondervan Publishing
House.

Library of Congress Cataloging-in-Publication Data

Coleman, William L.
    Before the ring : questions worth asking / William L. Coleman ;
illustrations by Ron Wheeler. — Rev. and expanded ed.
        p.   cm.
    ISBN 1-57293-036-5
    1. Dating (Social customs).   2. Interpersonal relations.   3. Dating
(Social customs)—Religious aspects—Christianity. I. Title.
HQ801.C67   1998
646.7'7—dc21   98-11309
                                                                       CIP

Printed in the United States of America

98 00 02 03 01 99
/ CHG /
1 3 5 7 9 10 8 6 4 2

Contents

Preface

FOR YEARS I HAVE TALKED TO COUPLES: married couples, divorced couples, remarried couples, engaged couples, and dating couples. Most have generously shared their good experiences and their dismal memories. I'm grateful for their willingness to open up and tell others what they have learned.

I believe that most people would marry the same person again. But I am just as convinced that if they could, they would go about it differently. They would learn more, grow more, ask more questions, reveal more of themselves, and argue less.

My hope for this book is that it will encourage couples thinking about engagement to take time to discuss some lasting issues. When couples take the time to get to know each other better, most will love one another all the more. They will become filled with the greatest gift God has given.

While I was writing this book, our daughter Mary received an engagement ring from Gerry. They're a great couple. We wish them every joy and happiness and pray that they will meet all the challenges ahead with courage and love. My special appreciation goes to Mary for reading this material and making helpful suggestions.

Chapter 1

Why So Many Questions?

IF YOU WERE PLANNING a two-week trip through the Rocky Mountains, you would ask hundreds of questions. What's the best way to get there? What will the weather be like? What clothes should I take? How much will it cost? Where will I stay? How many places will I be able to visit along the way?

When you are contemplating a trip that is to last the rest of your life, how foolish not to ask just as many or more questions before starting out.

Before you head off on vacation, you will want to ask questions about your car to make sure it is in good repair. Do the tires have plenty of tread, or are they bald and about to blow out? Has the engine been serviced regularly, or does it take a quart of oil a week to keep it running? Are the brakes in good shape, or do they squeal every time you touch them?

Even though the car runs well around town, you know that's no guarantee it will withstand mile after mile of mountainous driving. You have confidence in the car for small jaunts, but you have sense enough to know it needs extra attention before taking it on a long trip.

If you find some small defects, you can have them fixed before you hit the road. If you find major problems, you might want to find another vehicle to make the trip.

Asking questions about your car doesn't mean it's ready for the junk heap; it just means you want it in the best condition possible for the dangerous roads ahead. And asking questions about your relationship doesn't indicate you've given up on it; it just means you want to make sure it's not going to break down when you have to go through rough times.

The difficult thing about assessing a relationship is knowing which questions to ask and how to evaluate the answers.

"I knew Andy had a bad temper, but I figured he would settle down," Judy explained. "I had no idea it would turn to this. It's gotten so bad I'm afraid to talk to him."

The sad thing is that everyone knew but Judy. Her friends, her parents, and her minister all had serious questions about Andy's anger, but no one wanted to interfere. Judy may have saved herself some serious grief if she had known what to ask.

Listen to Chuck. "I wanted her body more than anything else in the world. When you're eighteen, you just sorta go nuts. I never even thought about things like goals or honesty or any of that stuff. I wanted to get married and go to bed. A lotta guys are like that."

And many of those who married the wrong person passed up a few "right" ones along the way simply because they failed to collect appropriate information.

"I should have married Jason," Amy said after her first marriage failed, "but like a dope I didn't know what love was. I pushed him away because he seemed too good."

A checklist

Everyone needs a checklist of values and character traits that he or she considers important when considering a marriage partner. Those who are Christians are concerned about putting their faith to work in selecting a mate, and the Bible lists certain traits that are essential elements of love. Among them are patience, kindness, trust, hope, perseverance; the absence of pride, boasting, and anger.

If neatness is a minor virtue to you, leave it off your list. If ambition is only a side issue, don't bring it up. But to ignore thinking about those values is to make no decision at all.

The best way to be sure of making a wise decision is to put your concerns into questions and discuss them fully. No list of values or set of questions, regardless of how thorough, will guarantee a perfect marital journey, but they will certainly make it more likely.

Not equal questions

This book suggests some questions to ponder. Years of observation and experience have shown me what issues young couples stumble over most often.

Not all questions are of equal importance. Some aren't important at all. You might not care whether your spouse is a Republican or a Democrat, but a Communist could be another matter. That's for you to decide.

Will socks on the floor drive you bonkers? How about lying? Can you tolerate someone who buries money in a coffee can in the backyard or one who spends it like confetti? Can you have a deep, enduring relationship with someone who considers Christ more like a wall plaque than a vital part of life?

You must determine the priority of your questions. They have to be your concerns and not the idle wondering of a third party. Just remember, a marriage that violates your values is headed for trouble.

Not pass/fail

The goal of asking these questions is not to see if you both pass the test. Your first and major purpose is to improve your relationship by discussing what is important to both of you. Tell each other what drives you up a wall and be honest enough to acknowledge potential trouble spots.

Practice the art of healthy dialogue before marriage and you will find it easier to do so on the other side of the altar. Openness, disclosure, and sharing are difficult for some, so you need to learn to express yourselves as early as possible.

Timing

The most important time to raise these issues is now. Don't wait until after you are engaged or married to discover that something is unsolvable.

There is little likelihood that you will change much after you marry. Meaningful adjustments are more apt to occur while you are still trying to win and impress each other. If they don't, watch out.

If you could start your marriage with five dollars for every heartbroken, tear-drained young person who has said, "Well, we just never talked about that before we got married," you could live comfortably without ever having to work.

UNRESTRAINED EXPRESSIVE
CANDOR - CHECK!

The fun of discovery

There is no reason to fear getting to know someone better. Every person is worth knowing, and many are terrific people filled with great character and amazing strength. Your initial positive instincts are usually verified when you get to know a person better.

Likewise, you have little to fear by allowing yourself to be known, by letting out your real feelings. Most of us are treasure chests with more jewels inside than we realize.

Everyone wants to marry someone who looks good. That is the major interest of most young couples. But beneath appearance must be character that won't fall apart under every little pressure. The point of meaningful questions is to test the strength of that character.

> *A wife of noble character who can find? She is worth far more than rubies. Her husband has full confidence in her and lacks nothing of value.*
>
> PROVERBS 31:10–11

Certainly it's possible you will conclude that Handsome Hank is really Hank the Horrible. But if so, better now than after signing a marriage license.

Enjoy getting to know each other.

Getting to know you ♥

1. What questions could Judy have asked to find out the seriousness of Andy's temper problem?

2. What questions could Chuck have asked to determine whether love or lust was his motive for marriage?

3. What questions could Amy have asked to learn whether Jason's good nature was indeed too good to be true?

4. Read 1 Corinthians 13 and list the qualities that make up love. List any others that are important to you (for example, neat, hardworking, smart, creative).
   What questions can you ask to determine whether or not your relationship has the qualities that will enable it to survive the long journey of marriage?

CHAPTER 2

So What's the Hurry?

How do you know when infatuation is growing into love? How can you tell if the early excitement you feel will develop into caring? One of the sure signs of love is an increasing patience with each other.

Patience isn't one of the characteristics we ordinarily think of when we discuss young love. Phrases like *impetuous, can't wait,* or *love at first sight* come to mind when we hear about a young couple considering marriage. It's almost as if there is a law that says true love is impatient.

Not so. Genuine love is characterized by patience.

If love is real, it has time to slow down and examine itself. Love takes time to ask what is best for each person involved, not just today but in the future as well. If you are in too much of a hurry, what you feel is probably another four-letter word that begins with *L: lust.* A relationship fueled by lust will last about as long as a piece of dynamite with a lit fuse.

*L**ove is patient.*

1 CORINTHIANS 13:4

Patience is one of the primary evidences we have that, given the right fuel, a relationship can last a long time.

Before you consider engagement, determine whether either of you has a problem with impatience and consider where that problem will lead you—one, two, or five years from now. The lack of patience is evidenced by the following:

- One pushes to do things the other doesn't want to do.
- One is accelerating the physical relationship faster than the other is comfortable with.
- One demands the other make decisions immediately.
- One establishes the timetable and the other must follow.
- One is under pressure a great deal of the time.
- One wants the relationship to be "more spontaneous."
- One is expected to be available whenever the other calls.

How many of those seven traits are true in your relationship? What percentage of the time are they true? Let's consider the subject from another angle. Check this list to see how patient your partner is.

- Does your sweetheart remain unperturbed when you want to spend the evening alone or with other friends?

- Does he or she tell you to take your time making up your mind?
- Does your dearest say, "We won't do anything about this until you are ready"?
- Is she or he willing to delay marriage until you receive the approval of family?
- Does he or she usually give you ample warning before you go someplace together?

These signs of thoughtfulness indicate that you are dealing with a patient person.

Immediate satisfaction versus long-range satisfaction

Before sealing your pledge with an engagement ring, ask if you are sacrificing the future in your haste to grab the present moment. Many couples who enjoy a great first six months of marriage spend the next six years in agony.

The Bible shares some excellent wisdom:

> *The end of a matter is better than its beginning, and patience is better than pride.*
>
> ECCLESIASTES 7:8

A relationship that will improve over time must have a solid foundation from the beginning.

Some people excel at dating and superficial relationships. They enjoy partying, socializing, flirting, giving presents, making small talk, and joking around.

The same people may have serious trouble handling conflict and may run from situations that require honest reflection and interaction.

Impatient people grab good daters and head for the altar. They believe the proverb that says He who hesitates is lost. When they find people they like, they don't want to risk losing them. This is not a good proverb to follow when considering marriage. A better one is Patience is the key of joy, but haste is the key of sorrow. Marriages that begin with fireworks may end up as scattered ashes.

If you've ever tried to build a campfire, you know the importance of using seasoned wood. Green wood (or recently cut wood) does not burn well. It makes a lot of smoke but never a roaring fire. Seasoned wood, on the other hand, gives warmth.

The same is true of relationships. A green relationship does not burn well because it hasn't been seasoned. Only time and experience can season a relationship.

How much time does it take to establish a good relationship? Who can say? Only the people involved can know. No one can tell you how long it takes to get to know each other.

Patience and the quality of a relationship

Patience involves far more than waiting to set the wedding date. Over the years patience will have a great deal to do with the fiber of your relationship.

"When Don wants an answer, he wants it right now," Gail grumbled. *"He may have thought about his plan for days, certainly for hours, but when he pops it on me, I have ten min-*

*utes to make up my mind. And I had better agree with his plan,
I can tell you that."*

People who are impatient create panic in the people
around them. They're like a fire alarm. When they have the
spark of an idea, their sirens blare, urgently insisting that
everyone move immediately.

Urgent personalities keep everyone in an uproar. They
are difficult people to live with because they expect everyone
else to share their concept of time. They do not allow others
the privilege of thinking things over.

Patient people are less likely to cause panic. They
smooth troubled waters by respecting the people they love.

The Scriptures say, "A patient man calms a quarrel"
(Proverbs 15:18).

A patient person encourages others to grow.

Good life partners make their spouses part of the program. They don't callously dump their own personal goals on
others.

Patient people take time to plan their vacations together.
They encourage each other to think things over and to contribute
personal feelings, hopes, and convictions to the discussion.
Impatient partners steamroll their mates.

Impatience creates anger, resentment, and bitterness.
You can count on it. Impatience is a form of contempt, and
eventually the beleaguered partner perceives it as exactly that.

*"If Rod had let me learn to fish at my own speed," Ellie said
with frustration, "I would probably still be going to the lake with
him. But he wanted me to do everything right now and do it cor-*

rectly. I baited the hook wrong. I held the line too tight. When I didn't catch anything, he made fun of me. So I don't go anymore."

Patient with self

While you are getting to know each other, make a few mental notes about how you each treat yourselves. Are you both patient or do you mercilessly berate yourselves when you make a mistake?

People who have no patience with themselves probably lack patience with others. And if they demand perfection from themselves, they will expect it from their mates and offspring. This can cause tremendous grief.

SOMEHOW I DON'T THINK YOU'RE AS PATIENT
WITH THIS RELATIONSHIP AS I AM, HELEN.

Patience and the Spirit

Patience is one of the fruits of the Spirit (see Galatians 5:22), and the good news is that God will help us gain patience if we want it.

When we allow Jesus Christ to control us, He dramatically alters our values. Incidents that formerly caused us to fly off the handle no longer get such explosive reactions. God helps us appreciate what is really important in life and in relationships.

Don't sit around and think about patience. Discuss it. Explain to each other what makes you impatient and ask for help to improve. Encourage each other to share experiences. Of what are you most tolerant and what makes you edgy and nervous? How can you help each other?

Patience isn't like height—something you either have or don't have. You can learn patience, improve it as a skill, and create a stronger relationship.

Getting to know you ♥

1. How would you describe your level of patience?

2. How would you describe the patience of the person you care about?

3. How can you begin to change if necessary?

4. What can you do to help yourself concentrate more on long-range satisfaction and less on immediate gratification?

CHAPTER 3 ♥

Opening Up the Treasure Chest

YOU'VE BECOME SPECIAL FRIENDS. You like what you see, enjoy what you know. You are eager to explore each other's treasure chest of character and find out more. But how can you each get the other to unlock the box and reveal what's inside?

This isn't easy. If one of you starts digging for what's at the bottom instead of first examining items on top, the other might slam the lid. If one gets too nosy, the other might crawl into the box, close the lid, and keep the key! You need to find loving ways to allow each other the freedom to express thoughts, feelings, and convictions in a comfortable setting.

Soul Contact

The word *intimacy* often serves as a euphemism for sexual intercourse. More accurately, however, it means "soul contact." It is communication at the deepest level. Intimacy not only strengthens a relationship, it also dramatically strengthens individual lives; it reduces loneliness, self-centeredness, and feelings of false guilt; it increases ability to trust, sense of worth, and feelings of saneness. It helps us accept the forgiveness of Christ.

Knowing it all

All of us know people who never have a private thought. Terry was one of those people. Friends frequently heard him say, "I say what I think. I don't like to be around people who don't say what they think."

Terry took this view of life a step farther. He demanded that people close to him reveal everything on their minds. Whenever his girlfriend wanted to keep her thoughts to herself or simply think something over for a while, Terry interrogated her like an ancient inquisitor. To protect herself she gradually said less and less, and her reserve grew deeper and deeper.

People are so complex, intriguing, and marvelous that we will never get to know everything about anyone. It would be like trying to understand the universe. There are too many parts, all in a continuous state of change, to ever comprehend it all. In this life we will not completely know each other, so be realistic in your goals. Some aspects of character and personality will remain unfathomable to each other. Because human beings are dynamic rather than static, new mysteries will develop over the years. The more you learn about your partner, the more there will be to learn.

Those who demand to know everything immediately are likely to remain ignorant forever.

Two kinds of questions

After enjoying a fun evening with friends, Matt and Sarah were sitting on the couch joking about some things that happened at the party. Suddenly Matt changed the topic of conversation to something more serious. "Your relationship to your mother is very important to our relationship," he announced. "So I need to know exactly how you feel about her. You aren't afraid to tell me, are you?"

Matt was hoping to get Sarah to speak honestly about a complex and difficult subject. Sarah wasn't ready. She had little idea how she really felt about her mother. By demanding to know, Matt scared her into silence.

Some questions, like the one Matt asked, are guaranteed to put a lid on communication. The following types of questions discourage meaningful interaction:

Accusing: "You can't communicate with women, can you?"

I'M NOT BEING TOO NOSY, AM I?

Quizzing: "How much money did you pay for your car?"

Too narrow: "Do you like foreigners?"

Too wide: "Tell me all about yourself."

Close-ended: "What political party do you like?"

Boxed in: "I hate football, don't you?"

Questions that promote conversation

Fortunately for Matt, he can learn new ways to ask questions that encourage conversation and self-disclosure rather than hinder it.

The right kind of questions at the correct time are essential. The following questions encourage free expression. They also demonstrate respect. Their tone suggests acceptance and willingness to listen.

Open-ended: "What sports do you enjoy?"

Opinion-centered: "What kind of church service do you appreciate?"

Personal without probing: "What do you find most satisfying about your job?"

Sharing: "I enjoy light rock; what kind of music do you like?"

Releasing: "Have you thought about where you would like to live?"

Intimate: "What do you like most about your parents?"

Reflective: "How would you like to improve your job?"

If one person does all the talking in your relationship, something is wrong. Caring people want to hear the opinions of those they love, and people who feel genuine love and acceptance are not afraid to express their opinions. Both parties must talk and listen or neither will achieve understanding.

Getting to know you ♥

1. What kind of discussion starters do you use?

2. How can you improve the way you ask questions?

3. Practice this statement: "In the interest of a close, intimate relationship, I will tell _____ about my feelings toward _____ ."

CHAPTER 4 ♥

No More Silly Games

PEOPLE IN RELATIONSHIPS are often like children playing hide-and-seek. Neither wants to emerge before the other. But someone must make the first move. In a relationship, when one finally dares to speak of hopes, fears, anger, happiness, thankfulness, joy, and even bitterness, the other usually will feel free to do the same. Each will open up in direct proportion to the other's willingness to do so.

When you make yourselves vulnerable to each other, you invest in your relationship. Honesty begets honesty, and honesty today will yield benefits for decades.

The guilt trap

When we hide from intimacy we usually do so because of a sense of guilt or inadequacy. We hide who we really are. We fear that when we marry, our spouses will discover what we are really like and no longer love us. Mature love, however, accepts, understands, and even appreciates who the loved one is, as well as who she or he is becoming. So we must spend energy revealing our thoughts and feelings, not hiding them.

Not that it is easy. Those who have spent twenty years hiding can expect some difficulty reversing that habit.

Discuss the matter together. Commit yourselves to coming out of hiding, to knowing one another intimately. Risk being open. It won't be easy, so be patient and understanding. Your commitment to each other and to honesty will provide incentive.

The need to pretend

David was among the world's great pretenders. He loved to exaggerate. According to him, he had been an outstanding high school athlete, scholar, and orator. As an adult, he bragged about his job, his friends, his exploits. Like Willy Loman in Death of a Salesman, *David felt a need to be someone other than who he was. Each exploit was a little larger, a bit wilder, somewhat more dangerous than the actual occurrence.*

When David married, his young bride realized that the man she married was a stranger. Like an actor in a long-running show, he was unable to separate himself from the character he played.

Most people begin relationships with a certain amount of pretense—nicer talk, better dress, politer behavior, more kindness than normal. What is wrong with this? Not necessarily anything. But some who do this lose touch with reality. They try too hard to impress each other and forget who they are. After marriage they live in fear of being found out, so they redouble their efforts to pretend.

No one can keep the act going forever. And if the performance is too extreme and the play lasts too long, the curtain may fall with horrendous results. Let the actors leave the stage. Take off the makeup. Be yourselves. Get to know each other.

Pretense serves no useful purpose in a relationship. It is unreal, and the lack of reality can only hurt. It causes anxiety in the pretender, which causes anxiety in the partner. Hence, an anxious relationship.

I DON'T KNOW HOW TO BREAK THIS TO YOU, DEAR, BUT I'M REALLY NOT THE DEBONAIR MAN OF PRESTIGE AND POWER THAT I'VE PORTRAYED MYSELF TO BE.

The larger the gap between who you are and who you pretend to be, the greater the anxiety for both partners. If you want a deep and lasting relationship, you must remove your disguises as fully and as soon as possible. The earlier you do so, the more time you will have to get to know each other intimately.

Getting to know you ♥

1. What character strength are you most pleased with in yourself? After you've each chosen, discuss why you each chose as you did.

2. What character weakness would you most like to improve in yourself? After you've each chosen one, discuss ways you can help each other improve.

3. Finish the following sentence: "When it comes to opening up and discussing my feelings, I am like . . . ."

CHAPTER 5

Beware of Pumpkin Shells

A FAMILIAR NURSERY RHYME paints a picture of a possessive husband desperate to keep his wife at home:

> *Peter, Peter, pumpkin-eater,*
> *Had a wife, and couldn't keep her;*
> *He put her in a pumpkin shell,*
> *And there he kept her very well.*

All we know about this couple is that she wanted to get out and go places and he wanted to keep her home.

Peter may not have figured out the pumpkin-shell solution to his problems until well into marriage, but the seeds of his plan were around long before.

The signs of jealousy, overprotectiveness, and insecurity are almost always apparent before marriage. If Peter's wife had been alert to a few clues, she might have saved herself the agony of being cooped up in an oversized orange house of strange design.

In real life there are plenty of Peters. Adam was one of them. He always needed to confine and control Cindy. While they dated he developed clever ploys to disguise his possessiveness. He insisted that he needed her around because he wasn't feeling well or wanted her help with some project. Slowly he narrowed her circle of involvement and friends. Cindy was flattered by how much he loved and needed her, so she gave up friends, activities, and family ties to spend time with this charming guy.

After their wedding Adam saw no more need for cleverness and he lost interest in his own ploys. He wanted Cindy home all the time, and he told her in no uncertain terms when and for what reasons she could leave the house.

Cindy was shocked by what she considered a sudden change in his personality. But Adam hadn't changed his personality at all; he just revealed his real one.

Cindy had spent four years earning a college degree and was planning a career in business, but Adam wouldn't allow her to work outside their home. He was afraid he would lose her if she led a life apart from him.

Ownership is selfishness

Few will defend selfishness as virtue. A relationship should satisfy both parties involved. No one need apologize for having received some benefit from a relationship, but problems arise when the major goal is self-fulfillment. Anyone who views the partner as a possession has crossed the line into self-centeredness.

Deep in our roots there remains more than a trace of the feeling that women are property, though we know this is neither healthy nor true. Confront any sense of ownership in your relationship. Marriage is a partnership, not an indenture of one party to the other.

Jealousy comes in different forms

There is more than one kind of jealousy, but only one type is legitimate. If your partner is unfaithful, you will feel, at the very least, angry, disappointed, betrayed. This type of jealousy is the kind God has for us when we allow someone or something to take His rightful place in our lives. It is normal and even healthy.

The second type of jealousy has no place in any relationship. The fabled green-eyed monster that hates to see another become too successful or too widely acclaimed or too popular will devour friendship from within.

Feelings of inferiority

Possessiveness, jealousy, and overprotectiveness often result from insecurity. Possessiveness gives one partner the feeling of control while making the other feel trapped and stifled.

Solomon describes jealousy as "unyielding as the grave" (Song of Songs 8:6). It holds on as stubbornly as earth holds a coffin. It may be flattering that someone wants to spend every moment with you, but never confuse possessiveness with love.

Pumpkin-shell prisons are created not only by men. Women can be just as possessive and jealous. Many men are controlled by the demands of their girlfriends and, later, by their wives.

A sixty-year-old man I know is wearing out faster than most men his age. Overweight, practically toothless, and without a decent set of clothes to his name, he is not likely to be called Casanova. But his wife worries day and night about his faithfulness. She badgers him about where he goes and whom he sees. Often she calls around town to make sure he has arrived where he said he was going.

Her need to put the clamps on her husband has no basis in fact. But her fears have become so exaggerated that she cannot separate reality from fantasy.

POSSESSIVE? HOW CAN YOU
CALL ME POSSESSIVE?

The statistics about extramarital affairs are alarming. But no one gets love or faithfulness by locking a partner in a shell. Faithfulness achieved by restraint is no sign of love. Love acknowledges individual will and grants choices. Love remains faithful out of internal desire not external control.

Feelings of superiority

An overdeveloped ego can be just as unhealthy as one that is underdeveloped. The amazing size of it may make it appear healthy, but it's not. A big ego is usually one that is out of control.

Although not limited to males, big egos may be more prevalent in men than in women. For example, the male ego often gets all puffed up by earning power, so a husband's ego is likely to suffer a bit if his wife's salary is larger than his.

It takes a man with a healthy ego—neither too small nor too large—to marry a woman who makes more money than he or one who gets more attention, more acknowledgment, or more promotions.

Feelings of equality

Jason and Tammy are about to get married. Each plans a professional career. She is a pharmacist and he is an accountant. They are bright, happy, and in love. They have worked hard to help each other reach their educational and professional goals.

So far there is no wrangling over who will make the most money. They can't conceive of making a major move without fully considering how it will affect the other's plans and career.

At this early stage each wishes the other the absolute best. Every accomplishment achieved by one will be celebrated by the other.

What will happen when life gets tough? If one is out of work or the other is promoted far more quickly, will this sweet reasonableness continue? No one knows for sure, but by the grace of God it will.

The most significant thing is that they started their relationship without jealousy. Each feels secure enough not only to wish the other well but even to support the other's ambitions.

Do you want to help each other reach goals? If not, remain friends but look for someone else with whom to spend the next fifty years. If your answer is yes, however, begin to discuss how to do so. Begin to plan how you will help each other fulfill personal and shared goals.

A person eager for you to become everything God wants you to be, not one eager for you to become everything he or she wants you to be, will make a wonderful spouse, and you won't have to worry about being locked up in a pumpkin shell for the rest of your life.

Getting to know you ♥

1. Do you wish your parents were more dependent on one another or more independent of one another? Explain.

2. What signs of possessiveness do you see in your own relationship? What can you do to overcome them?

3. Discuss how you each would feel if at some time in your marriage the wife earns a higher income than the husband.

CHAPTER 6

Going with a Perfectionist

WHENEVER SID MAKES A MISTAKE *he is very hard on himself. A misplaced tool causes his temper to flare. If he gets sick, Sid is disappointed that his body got a virus.*

This young man is a perfectionist. He believes that job, family, health, and relationship should all be totally under control. Nothing in his life should be out of place or unpredictable—not for long.

Sid's need for control makes him feel like a failure whenever something isn't perfect. Anything out of its slot, place, or drawer bothers him tremendously.

What's wrong with this? Doesn't he sound like every mother's dream son-in-law? He is responsible, hardworking, and dependable. How much could a person mess up in life if he or she is a perfectionist?

Trying the impossible

The biggest problem with Sid is that he is trying to do what can't be done. Perfectionism in this life is impossible. And when we try to do the impossible, we almost always hurt ourselves and others.

If a husband comes home and tells his wife he is going to take a running leap across the Grand Canyon, certain truths are immediately obvious. One, he will hurt himself very badly. Two, the emergency room at the local hospital should be notified. Three, his wife should immediately take out a large insurance policy.

PERFECTIONIST? I'M NOT A PERFECTIONIST. THERE ARE LOTS OF GUYS WHO IRON THEIR UNDERWEAR.

Not only will he get hurt, but the people closest to him are going to be hurt, too.

Perfectionists imagine they can control everything around them. Their goals are not noble or idealistic. Their goals are dangerous.

A sense of inadequacy

Why would someone have the unrealistic goal of trying to be perfect? Often it is because the person feels seriously inadequate. If I am not in control, I am afraid I cannot adequately respond to changing circumstances. The fear of change drives a person to perfectionism.

Perfectionism grows out of an inner weakness. A perfectionist cannot tolerate loose ends.

Does the Bible tell us to be perfect?

Does the Bible tell us to be perfect? Many Christians get all twisted out of joint over this. When they see the word *perfect,* all kinds of alarms light up and begin to ring. But there is a vast differ-

> *Aim for perfection, listen to my appeal.*
>
> 2 CORINTHIANS 13:11

ence between someone who aims for perfection and someone who is a perfectionist.

Suppose a young man enjoyed doing woodwork. For weeks he worked hard to make a cedar chest for his mother.

> *To all perfection*
> *I see a limit;*
> *but your commandments*
> *are boundless.*
>
> PSALM 119:96

His goal was to make an excellent chest, something his mother would be proud of. This man is an artisan.

A second man, a perfectionist, also builds a cedar chest for his mother.

When each one finished, he turned his chest over for one last inspection.

The first man found a mistake on the bottom of the chest. He was disappointed. The next time, he resolved, he would not make the same mistake. Soon he smiled and delivered the work to his appreciative mother.

The second young man turned over his finished work and saw a similar mark on the bottom. The perfectionist began to curse himself, throw tools around the room, and tell himself he was useless.

In disgust the perfectionist tossed the chest into the corner of the room to store nails in. He then went out to purchase a present for his mother.

Each young man had exactly the same worthy goal of building a piece of furniture. However, one could be content with a good effort and the other was devastated under the burden of perfectionism.

Those who think they should do everything perfectly are in for enormous pain. Those who know how to accept limits will be content.

Perfectionism is performance-centered

How would you rate the person you are getting serious about? How would you rate yourself? Does either of you feel important only when you do a terrific job? Do you need an outstanding position or fabulous career in order to believe you really count? If so, you rate the importance of individuals by their performance or the product they make or the money they earn.

Do you think a bank president is more important than a baby-sitter? Are brain surgeons more important then telemarketers? If the answer to either of these is yes, try this one: Is a child who can run more important than a child in a wheelchair?

Most people who think they are valuable because of what they do also believe other people are less valuable. That conclusion is almost inevitable.

If you marry a perfectionist, you marry someone who might think housewives, waiters, and mechanics are less valuable. You may marry someone who thinks she or he is better than you.

The Bible sees us as of equal value. It would certainly be good if the person you marry saw everyone of equal value. After all, God created us all in His image.

An obsession

Perfectionism is usually not quick to heal itself. Don't assume that someone will mature and grow out of it. Someone who is extremely harsh on self and on others may suffer from a deep problem.

The best thing to do is to talk about it early. Ask questions and wait for answers. Never assume that this personality trait won't affect you. Unchanged, this problem could have a profound effect on you and your children.

The following list highlights traits to look for and discuss. They might be found in you. They could be found in the person you care about.

- Does one of you get upset about not winning games?
- Is one of you a person who doesn't play games—only competes?
- Does one of you believe he or she is better than others?
- Is one of you highly critical of the other or of other people?
- Does one of you have a strong need to be in control?
- Does one of you have trouble admitting faults?
- Does one of you tend to never change your mind?
- Is one of you angry when others make mistakes?

These eight tendencies do not prove you or your dearest suffers from perfectionism. However, they are so significant that you would do well to discuss them if they exist.

A higher standard than God's

God knows we make mistakes and loves us to the extent of giving His own Son. If God reserves His love and acceptance for perfect people, it's all over. None of us would qualify.

Perfectionists will nod their heads "Yes" to all of that and still feel a drive to be perfect. They believe it without really accepting it.

There is a price to pay when we set a standard higher than God's. Those who are driven to make work the most important thing in life become workaholics. Spirituality, family, leisure, and even love take a backseat to the tasks at hand.

While dating, perfectionists may be torn between love and work. The prize of winning a special person is a powerful draw. But don't be surprised if later it changes. Once the goals of engagement and marriage have been reached, they will be able to devote their energies to their number-one love: perfectionism and, ultimately, work.

Perfectionists will have trouble relaxing, listening, vacationing, waiting, serving others, if they see it as an obstacle to performing well at their important tasks. Consequently they will have difficulty with relationships.

Cross gender

Traditionally perfectionism and workaholism have been seen as male characteristics. This is no longer the case. Many women also see their lives as performance-centered.

Women or men who never rest or do other things may well be perfectionists who refuse to stop working and do more important things. There is a Bible narrative about Mary, Martha, and Jesus. Martha was so busy working that she could not let go and benefit from the teaching of Christ Himself.

> *In the image of God, he created him, male and female, he created them.*
>
> GENESIS 1:27

As women climb the business ladder, the temptation toward perfectionism increases. They may want perfect homes, families, and jobs. That obsession has consequences for everyone.

Talk it over

Take time to discuss values. Talk about what's important to each of you. How driven are you? What does success mean? How do you enjoy life when you aren't working? How important are your relationships? Does spirituality mean peace with God or simply another program? Would either of you sacrifice your relationship in order to become president of a company? Would you be happy to see your spouse work around-the-clock now and wait to enjoy each other when you are fifty-five?

> *G*odliness with contentment is great gain.
>
> 1 TIMOTHY 6:6

Excellence is a good idea. A person who cares for quality can be a well-rounded individual. Life at its best is lived with an appreciation for the spiritual side that Christ wishes to bring into our lives.

Getting to know you ♥

1. Is achievement or success the most important thing in your life?

2. When you got a B on a report card, did you feel like a failure?

3. Does either one of you have a strong need to be in control of the other?

4. Is either of you like Martha in the Bible story?

CHAPTER 7 ♥

Someone to Lean On

IF YOU KNEW KRISTI *you would understand why she married the character she did. Growing up, she saw her father as an undependable figure. Rather than interact with his family, he merely passed through it from time to time.*

Kristi learned to expect this behavior from men. She viewed them as untrustworthy, disconnected, and unaccountable. Kristi thought these were inherent male characteristics that were impossible to change. So it's no surprise that she married Tom, someone very much like her father. Tom prizes his independence and considers it an invasion of his privacy to have to tell Kristi who he is with, where he is going, or when he will be home.

The following statement may shock people who grew up in homes where the father acted like a visitor, but it's true. *Marriage partners are supposed to be trustworthy and dependable.* They are supposed to share and interact. Married people have no right to do whatever they want whenever they want. That's called being single.

Have you ever said to yourself: "I cannot trust the person I am dating, but that's all right because no one is trustworthy. After we're married I'll just keep my eyes open for signs of trouble."

If you have, warning bells should be clanging.

Every reliable person deserves a reliable partner.

First Corinthians 13, called the "love chapter" of the Bible, says that love "always trusts" (v. 7).

GOOD NEWS, DEAR. I'VE DECIDED TO BECOME TRUSTWORTHY AND DEPENDABLE.

This doesn't mean that we are to trust someone who is untrustworthy, unreliable, fickle, temperamental, or troublesome. That makes no sense.

Loving trust means that we believe each other. We have no reason to expect that our love will be betrayed and so we are not suspicious of each other.

Don't marry someone who needs a full-time detective. Marry to be a partner and a companion—not a watchdog.

Lean on me

One of the advantages of marriage is that each partner has someone to lean on during difficult times. On days and nights when you need additional support, when you need someone who cares, your spouse is there. A crisis would be a terrible time to find out your lover is part of the problem rather than the solution. Occasionally even the most reliable partner will fail in a crucial hour. But don't marry someone who lets you down most of the time.

Earn each other's trust

If you have expressed concern about your partner's trustworthiness and the only response you've gotten is, "If you love me, you must trust me," perhaps your response should be, "If I cannot trust you, I cannot love you."

The matter in question is not your capacity to trust. It's whether or not the person you want to trust is trustworthy.

When Lynne started to get on a ski lift she noticed a few defects, so she stepped back and looked it over. When she did, she saw that the lift was barely attached to the cable, the seat looked as if it were about to split in two, and the guardrail wasn't in position. So Lynne started looking for another way up the slope.

The attendant yelled after her, "Look, you have to show more trust. Don't be chicken. Jump on!"

His statement suggested there was something wrong with Lynne because she didn't trust a dilapidated, broken-down ski lift.

Some people might be foolish enough to give in to this type of argument and climb on to keep from looking like cowards, but those who do are giving in to danger. In a roundabout way, the ski attendant was saying Lynne could show her bravery by getting on his rickety lift.

In much the same way, an untrustworthy partner will make you think your capacity for love is greater if you trust him or her.

This is a faulty form of reasoning. The matter in question is trustworthiness, not the ability to trust.

Anyone who falls for this kind of logic will land with a painful thud.

Inspiring trust

There is no reason to trust someone the first time you meet. Trust develops over time as a result of good experiences. It is not an act of blind faith.

But once you start developing a relationship, you should consciously do things that inspire trust in one another. In both of your lives there should be evidence (solid proof, not empty promises) of trustworthiness.

Jesus said, "Whoever can be trusted with very little can also be trusted with much, and whoever is dishonest with very little will also be dishonest with much" (Luke 16:10).

Are both of you trustworthy in small things? Do you keep promises and commitments? If you have established a pattern of trustworthiness in small things, there is good reason to believe you are trustworthy in important things as well.

Never test deceitfully

Some people run wild with plots to test a partner's trustworthiness. They enlist friends to check up on their partners' activities. Some even try to cause jealousy simply to gauge the reaction.

The proof of trustworthiness should come out of ordinary, everyday living, not out of any wild scheme. Don't set traps or develop elaborate tests. Simply keep your eyes and ears open and be willing to accept reality. Promises of trustworthiness have no meaning apart from actions.

Look for patterns of behavior. Does exaggeration border on lying? Are some activities off-limits to discussion?

We can calculate how far away lightning is by watching the flashes of light in the sky and counting the seconds until the thunder rolls. The test for trust is similar. By determining the distance between what a person says and what that person actually does, we can judge honesty. Measure the distance between what you say and what you do. The two should be extremely close. If you talk about loyalty, commitment, and dependability but are slow in showing them, you have a dependability gap that makes a serious relationship with you a dangerous risk.

Excuses, excuses

Danny doesn't always keep his word, Kristen explains, but that's because he has a lot on his mind. He often works late and sometimes he needs to get away and blow off steam. "I understand why he forgets to call and let me know," she says. "He's still young. As he grows up, he'll settle down and become more dependable. I've seen it happen lots of times."

Kristen wants to believe the best and is willing to stretch the truth to suit her needs. And she is correct about several things.

- Danny is young.
- He has a great deal of pressure.
- He will probably grow up.

At the same time she is ignoring other possibilities:

- Danny may not see the need to change.
- He might not be concerned about the gap between his word and his performance.
- He might be very slow in growing up.
- He may never grow up.
- Danny may not be mature enough to marry.

Kristen should be reluctant to marry Danny until his behavior causes her to trust him rather than make excuses for him. That isn't too much to ask.

A sense of confidence

Nearly everyone appreciates some spontaneity, a bit of unpredictableness. But that is not the same as having a spouse you can't count on.

The virtuous woman in Proverbs 31 is star-studded with outstanding character. One of her most prized qualities is her trustworthiness.

This isn't a gender-related quality. Both male and female should fully expect to rely on one another.

> *Her husband has full confidence in her and lacks nothing of value.*
>
> PROVERBS 31:11

From that foundation a couple can build a lasting and loving marriage. If you cannot yet put full confidence in each other, slow down the relationship. Don't gamble. I promise you, it isn't worth the risk.

Getting to know you ♥

Ask the following questions about yourself. Then ask them about your partner and discuss your responses.

1. Do you keep your word?

2. Do you show up on time?

3. Do you pay your bills?

4. Do you call when you say you will?

5. Do you like to act secretively?

6. Do you like to confuse your partner?

7. Do you disappear when you're needed?

8. Do you avoid responsibilities?

CHAPTER 8 ♥

Life in the Gender Blender

AS LITTLE BOYS, my friends and I used to kid about how glad we were that we weren't girls. The truth is we were only half kidding. While we didn't really believe in "girl germs" or that girls were dumb, we did consider them inferior.

As we grew older some of us came to see females as nearly equal, but few of us learned to see women as equal.

The emergence of "superior" women who tout female as better than male has added greater confusion to these changing attitudes. Such women have a long list of emotional, mental, and spiritual strengths they claim clearly outshine any male traits.

It's tough living in the gender blender. Men hesitate to offer a seat on the subway to a pregnant women for fear of getting reprimanded. Women are afraid to bake cookies for the office party lest they look too domestic and get called "Honey."

All of this could be considered mere social tension if not for the fact that millions are getting hurt. One of the places we see the most pain is in the home. Couples chewed up in the gender blender end up in messy divorces. Other couples, while avoiding divorce, struggle because both feel as though they are stuck in stereotypical roles.

Gender roles must be near the top of the list of vital issues young couples discuss. And *discuss* is the key word. Don't expect agreement if your communication tools are hammers. You can't get someone to agree with you by pounding away. Take time with each other. Gently wipe away the layers of prejudice and take a close look at attitudes, values, feelings, and potential.

I'D OFFER YOU MY SEAT BUT I DON'T WANT TO OFFEND YOUR SENSE OF EQUALITY.

Care enough to help each other be objective. Don't lose your patience at the first prejudicial, antiquated, misinformed statement and say, "Well, if that's the way you feel . . . ." Your relationship is worth the extra time and energy it takes to come to agreement on difficult but important issues.

Cuts both ways

Attitudes of gender superiority aren't exclusively a male phenomenon. The reverse is often true. Many women have had miserable experiences with men and consider males the inferior sex. Some remember prejudiced fathers, teachers, pastors, brothers, or boyfriends who treated them as second-class people. Others had bitter mothers or aunts who had sour attitudes toward anyone male.

A great transformation happened in Courtney's life. She grew up with an abusive, heavy-drinking father and ended up with an almost identical husband. When her forty-five years of living with miserable men ended in an ugly divorce, Courtney was disillusioned and angry at the entire male population.

By the grace of God she eventually became a Christian and met a caring, middle-aged man who treated her with love and respect. Courtney risked loving again, and the chiseled look on her face gradually changed into a relaxed, joyful smile.

Don't be surprised if one of you has a certain amount of hesitancy and distrust. Stereotypes and foul encounters have left a great number of people gender shy. But with patience we are able to move toward each other with mutual appreciation.

The goal is to help each other get beyond any form of gender bashing.

A virtuous woman

While teaching a class on the virtuous woman of Proverbs 31, I made note of the fact that she went out, considered a piece of land, and bought it. I pointed out that the woman obviously had considerable freedom if she could make the decision and buy a plot of land.

A man in the fourth row leaped to his feet. That couldn't be the case, he insisted. Even though the text didn't mention consultation with her husband, the man knew she wouldn't dare buy land without permission.

He knew it because he couldn't comprehend that kind of liberty in his own marriage. He had never seen it, never even heard of it, and couldn't imagine that any God-fearing male would allow it to happen.

Prejudices have long and productive lives. Unfortunately, what they produce is harmful. Our best chance of correcting them is through love and patience.

What to talk about?

> *There is neither Jew nor Greek, slave nor free, male nor female, for you are all one in Christ Jesus.*
>
> GALATIANS 3:28

As you discuss the gender gap, use some biblical principles as guidance.

1. *Paul's equality principle.*

For Christians there should be no gender gap. Every male and female stands before God on the same playing field. Boys are no more important than girls. Sons are not more to be desired than daughters.

Despite this declaration of equality, some parents are disappointed when their firstborn child is a girl. Mothers as well as fathers often feel this way. Others have overreacted and consider daughters to be of more value than sons. Neither position is healthy for parents or children.

If either of you grew up in a home where one of the sexes was elevated and the other downgraded, you have the opportunity for some interesting discussion and exploration.

The solid Christian principle is that male and female are of equal value in God's eyes.

Paul wasn't calling for unisex. Women still bear children and men don't. Men still produce sperm and women carry ova. Both are equal in value and should be treated with equal respect and love.

The concept of first- and second-class people is not biblical in origin. These are erroneous distinctions we made up on our own.

Everyone has prejudices, so don't expect to find someone without any. But a good marriage partner will acknowledge her or his prejudices and will be open to change if those prejudices are proven to be human rather than God-given in origin.

2. *Christ's protection principle.*

Historically, men have controlled most forms of government and religious institutions. As a result, women have been at a decided disadvantage. They have been dependent on men to define and defend their rights. This lack of balance might be changing as more women enter public life, but tra-

> *I tell you that anyone who divorces his wife, except for marital unfaithfulness, and marries another woman commits adultery.*
>
> MATTHEW 19:9

ditionally men have had the upper hand.

Confronting that inequality, Jesus Christ took a huge step toward protecting the rights of women. In an era when men could divorce their wives for any reason but women could never divorce their husbands, Jesus protested the inequality. At the risk of offending tens of thousands of men Jesus told them they could not divorce their wives simply because they were tired of them.

He called for an end to the women-are-possessions philosophy. And he did it in the face of serious opposition.

When women are not in a position to stand up for their own rights, Christ stands up for them. God is interested in protecting wives, mothers, and widows from any system or philosophy that harms them.

3. *Christ's defense of women's minds.*

Few women were well educated in Jesus' day. Most were taught only to cook, clean, and raise children. Jesus invited them to learn even the most complex subjects.

In the narrative about Martha and Mary the contrast is clear. Martha busied herself with traditional female chores. She buzzed around preparing treats and tidying up. After some time, tired of doing all the work, she asked Christ to tell Mary to get up and help her with the preparations in the kitchen.

Instead of doing as she asked, Christ told Martha that Mary had made a better choice. Mary was listening and learning, expanding her mind and soul. That was more important than making biscuits and spreading cheese.

On many occasions Christ showed respect for women with intellectual and spiritual interests. He knew they could do more than fold clothes and make centerpieces.

4. *The biblical call to minister.*

Some have serious questions about women ministering to men, but Scripture teaches and illustrates women engaged in ministry to people in all walks of life.

Philip had four daughters who prophesied (Acts 21:9). Paul expressed his gratitude to the many women who touched his life through their special ministries (Romans 16:1 and following). And the early church saw many women involved in serving Jesus in a number of significant capacities (Matthew 26:6–7).

Explore the subject of ministry. Develop concepts and suggest ways you could work as a team as well as separately.

My wife and I are involved in similar ministries. She works with one group and I meet with the other. We then compare notes, make suggestions, and return to those separate responsibilities.

There is a vast variety of ways a couple can minister. Begin by molding attitudes. How does each of you see this part of your Christian experience? Will the male in your relationship expect women to limit their service to nursery duty? Is he uncomfortable seeing a woman in a leadership role outside the home?

The leader of a growth group I attend is a woman. Her husband is also involved in the group in a supportive role and has no problem letting her play the major part. As a couple they are at ease with her ability to minister.

Don't find out later that he thinks your role in Christian ministry is limited to making chicken casserole for the church potluck. Don't learn a year from now that she believes your role is to escort her to rallies where she campaigns for her favorite Christian cause.

5. *The biblical principle of priesthood.*

Peter described Christians as royal priests. Our function as priests is to give witness that God is working in our lives. There is no gender qualification for this priesthood. The Old Testament rules of priesthood do not apply. Members of the royal priesthood are those who know Christ, and their job is to give testimony to His reality. Men and women, boys and girls, grandmothers and grandfathers can carry out that function.

> *You are a chosen people, a royal priesthood, a holy nation, a people belonging to God, that you may declare the praises of him who called you out of darkness into his wonderful light.*
>
> 1 PETER 2:9

Priests offer sacrifices to God. Those sacrifices are (1) praising God and (2) doing good and sharing with others (Hebrews 13:15–16). There is no gender gap in this duty and privilege.

Reach deeply into each other's hearts and find out what is going on. Then help each other grow and become even more understanding.

Equals, mothers, children, and teens

Alan knew exactly what he wanted in a wife. He wanted his mother. She did everything right. Mother cooked, cleaned, told him when to leave and when to come home. She even made calls to get her boy out of trouble.

Now he wanted a girl who was just like dear old Mom.

For every man looking to marry a mother-type, there is also a female searching for a father-type. The problem is that parent-child relationships usually make terrible marriages.

Ask yourself where this relationship is going: Are you

1. *Mother or father?*

Must one of you be dependent on the other? Is one the responsible person while the other needs to be prodded and told what to do?

Unfortunately, some mates want the parent role as much as the other wants to be parented. Reject either role.

2. *Big babies?*

Too often marriage partners act like two babies. They hold their breath, stick their tongues out, and frequently try to get even. These relationships look more like sibling battles than actual marriages.

3. *Jealous teens?*

Adolescent children continually fight over the bathroom. They argue about the TV, they correct each other, and compete for attention.

Marriage partners who constantly struggle over which show to watch or who gets the remote are still trying to complete their teen revolution. We all need to find peace with ourselves before we marry.

4. Equals?

Is each person of equal value and do you treat the other as an adult? Do you show the same respect as you would another adult at work or at church? Marriage should only be for equals.

Quickly move toward becoming an adult who is willing to accept others as adults, too.

Getting to know you ♥

1. Discuss how each of you understands the roles of males and females in ministry and in marriage.

2. Do men and women understand art, politics, religion, business, and finances in the same way?

3. What are some ways you can help each other see the full spectrum of the physical, spiritual, and intellectual abilities God gives us?

CHAPTER 9

Dreams, Desires, Goals, Ambitions

DREAMS ARE ALWAYS SUBJECT TO CHANGE but that doesn't keep us from dreaming. Desires change frequently, but that doesn't keep us from buying an item we want at a particular moment. Goals and ambitions are likewise subject to change, but that is no reason to consider them unimportant.

"I knew Robert wanted to be a missionary, but I thought that was just a childish dream," Angela explained to her marriage counselor. "I was sure I could convince him to go into business after we were married. If I had known I would spend my whole life in poverty I never would have married him."

A couple considering marriage needs to know what is important to each other. What attitudes and values control your life? Are you concerned about wealth? popularity? education? service to others? service to God?

Such goals and ambitions tell us far more about each other than we can learn by discussing what kind of car we prefer and where we want to live.

Goals and ambitions come from our hearts. They are the energy that keeps us going, the thread that holds us together. And ultimately they will determine our success or failure.

The Bible gives excellent measuring rods to evaluate a person's ambitions. One of them says, "The plans of the righteous are just" (Proverbs 12:5).

Another way of saying it is that good people do not conjure up evil and selfish plans. Righteous people do not claw

YER RIGHT, MA. I'DA BEEN A BETTER HUSBAND
IF'N I WEREN'T SO BLINDED BY AMBITION.

and cheat their way to the top. Committed followers of Christ will not visualize the cottage by the bay and do anything to get it. To do so would be to compromise their highest value: dedication to the Son of God.

Blinded by ambition

Ambition is not a dirty word. Ambition means you set targets and try to hit them. Whether your target is to feed the hungry or to be president of General Motors doesn't matter; both can be hon-

> *Where you have envy and selfish ambition, there you find disorder and every evil practice.*
>
> JAMES 3:16

orable. The question is whether either ambition is so powerful that it blinds you to the more important priorities of life.

I have seen Christians lead growing ministries while consumed by personal ambition.

William Henry Davies wrote:

> *I had Ambition,*
> *By which sin the Angels fell;*
> *I climbed and, step by step, O Lord,*
> *Ascended into Hell.*

If a person's career means more than family or faith, a prospective spouse should know that. If your definition of a successful life is to acquire a million dollars, your prospective spouse should know that interesting tidbit. Both should be aware of the intensity, dedication, and sacrifice the other is willing to invest in the pursuit of personal goals.

What forces drive you? Is either of you unable to see the better part of life because you are blinded by the temporary and the meaningless?

Thousands of people create families and then pursue careers that allow no room for those families. They work day and night to build successful empires while their families founder and fail. If either of you has that type of ambition, you owe it to one another to admit it before marriage.

Individuals who are driven by personal goals and selfish plans make terrible life partners. If you're planning to fly a one-seater airplane your whole life, you have no business asking someone to be your copilot.

The moral isn't to look for a spouse with no ambition. The goal is to find someone who appreciates your goals and ambitions and is willing to compromise to keep a fair and healthy balance between the two.

Clues to look for

Recently a young woman was convicted of embezzling three million dollars and now faces a possible twenty-year prison term. For a few years she and her husband enjoyed expensive clothes, cars, homes, and vacations.

Today her world of greed and deceit has collapsed and injured the people closest to her. Was she always deceptive? Were there early traces of ruthless ambition? Did anyone stand back and say, "Watch out; this woman will someday create big trouble"?

It doesn't take Sherlock Holmes to recognize a gun on the table or dynamite in the pantry. Many clues are that obvious.

1. Is money everything?

Bernie never saw people, only dollar signs. Some people were small dollar signs, others large dollar signs. Everyone was a potential deal, a possible sale, a contact for more business. People without money were a

> *T*he love of money is a root of all kinds of evil.
>
> 1 TIMOTHY 6:10

bother. He didn't get involved with them because they would only slow him down in his pursuit of money.

The loaded gun is on the table. If money is his driving force, anything that stands in his way, including family, is in danger. Only a fool will ignore an insatiable desire for wealth.

2. Is education everything?

What could be wrong with anything as worthwhile as education? When education is the all-compelling motivation, there can be a great deal of wrong in it.

> *I*f anyone does not provide for his relatives, and especially for his immediate family, he has denied the faith and is worse than an unbeliever.
>
> 1 TIMOTHY 5:8

Some people are not able to handle the stresses of college and a loving relationship at the same time. Too often the stress of classes, homework, and exams pulls couples apart.

Some goal-centered people put off love and involvement until they have acquired their basic degrees. They know what they want, and in what order.

These are not minor issues. Are you willing to marry a person who will devote the major part of the next four years to work and education and make your relationship of minor importance?

Some couples take this route and flourish. Others perish. Use education as a platform for discussion and see what has to be accomplished and at what cost to your relationship.

3. Is service everything?

Being married to the famous missionary David Livingstone was tough on Mary. Left to raise the children while her husband mapped and evangelized Africa, she must have felt the terrible burden of loneliness.

Some of us are attracted to this type of helping personality. Is one of you constantly off fixing someone else's plumbing, delivering groceries, baby-sitting for neighbors, or volunteering for committees? Is one of you drowning in Christian service and kindness? Is either of you the type that can't imagine spending a quiet evening at home when there are so many needs to be met?

If either of you thinks you can serve everyone in the world while ignoring the person you marry, start talking now. These serving types often do not believe that charity begins at home. They see devotion to their own families as an act of selfishness. These people need help in understanding a better balance of Christian love.

You can be passionate about your dreams, desires, goals, and ambitions as long as they are God-given and balanced.

Whatever your driving interests, you need to understand them, decide where your partner will stand in relationship to those pursuits, and then communicate that information so there is no misunderstanding about it after marriage.

And never, never buy the argument that absence is in your best interest. Your mutual best interests are that you will pursue your plans and lives together, not as tourists following separate guides.

One of the many pleasures of getting acquainted is learning to appreciate another person's goals and ambitions. Usually those discoveries make us want to know each other better. But sometimes they alert us to step back and rethink our involvement.

Good people have good goals. Never rationalize that a person is good if his or her goals are twisted and perverted. This is never the case. Selfish plans are made by selfish people. Vengeful plans are made by vengeful people. Greedy plans are made by greedy people. Good plans are made by good people.

> *Those who plan what is good find love and faithfulness.*
>
> PROVERBS 14:22

Where do you want to be and how do you want to get there? The destination may change but the way you get there will be determined by the kind of person you are.

Getting to know you ♥

1. What is the purpose of money?

2. Discuss whether or not you think it is possible to make too much money.

3. Of the money each of you earns now, what percentage do you spend on yourself? On others?

4. Do either of you have career goals that suggest one of you will be traveling a great deal? Discuss how this will affect your relationship. What if you have children, and one must stay home with them?

CHAPTER 10 ♥

Love on the Rebound

MARK AND KIM MET AT A SINGLES' PICNIC. *Mark proved to be a good softball player who could smash a long ball and run the bases well.*

For four straight nights afterward he called Kim. They went walking, had ice cream, and played miniature golf. Kim was more than flattered and her sister told her how happy she looked.

A week later, on their fifth date, Mark confided in her, "Tell me if you think I'm being too pushy. I don't mean to be. It's only that I went with this girl for over a year, and now that we've split, I really need someone like you to fill this terrible ache. I don't know how to explain it, but I am so lonely."

Hit the brakes! Stop the bus! This vehicle needs to slow down and pull over to the curb.

A lost relationship has left Mark with a hole in himself the size of a vacuum cleaner bag. Understandably he is in a mad rush to fill that void as soon as possible. The problem is that his determination to meet a need is probably going to cloud his judgment and could easily get a couple of people needlessly hurt.

High-risk choices

Often people are very vulnerable right after they lose someone through death, divorce, or a broken relationship. Their hearts may be broken; they feel abandoned and overwhelmed by the need to find another person to love them. In that condition they are unlikely to make sound decisions and good choices.

> *For I am poor and needy, and my heart is wounded within me.*
>
> PSALM 109:22

Unfortunately, they seldom appreciate how faulty their judgment has become. They are positive that the loss has no influence on their thinking process. Refusing to listen to anyone, they walk a tightrope and take their chances.

Sometimes it works. Some happy couples meet two weeks after a breakup and live well together for forty years. Many other lives turn into disasters because a couple found a relationship while rebounding.

In Mark's case he was looking for a woman, almost any woman, to fill the gap. He doesn't much care if it is Kim or Emily or Sondra, as long as it is a person to meet his need.

Kim may be excited at the attention, but she could also be sorry later.

The facts are that second marriages are high risk under most circumstances. Divorce rates are higher the second time around than they were the first. Exactly what the risk is among those who marry soon after a lost relationship we cannot be certain. But there is plenty of reason to look carefully before hurrying into a second situation.

Looking for love, a person, or a relationship?

Anyone recovering from loss might be uneasy about his or her motivation. Am I looking for love to fill the emptiness? If that is the goal, I may simply be in love with love, and the person I love is of little con-sequence. That's dangerous.

The cry is for someone to come and love me. I will treat you well if you come and love me.

Real shaky ground.

I have too little regard for who that person might

> *Rachel was lovely in form and beautiful. Jacob was in love with Rachel.*
>
> GENESIS 29:17–18

be. Love is blind enough as it is. When love is the only driving force, I am speeding down a highway at night with my head-lights off.

There is another possible goal, also mistaken. The sce-nario goes something like this:

"I need the right kind of person— someone who is a good cook, enjoys children, has a decent job, and is strong."

It's the kind of ad you might find in a personals section in the classifieds. Basically it's a job description.

Marriages of convenience refer to those where a couple may not necessarily be in love but they feel each has something to offer the other. One has a solid job. The other has parenting skills. One owns a house. The other is good at running a business. One sings. The other plays guitar.

After coming through a loss in relationship people think they know exactly what will meet their needs, and they have no time to waste. They must get on with the task of discovering the right partner.

A third possible goal, and the most difficult, is to establish a relationship and then see where it leads. The aim is relationship and not convenience or desperation.

Ideally, a marriage begins on mutual attraction, a fascination and appreciation with each other's personality, a taste of magic, charm, enticement, mutual faith, and a host of intangibles. No longer do we select partners on their ability to haul water from the well. It is reasonable to expect your mate to be attractive to you.

Back off and slow down

Brad and Jessica wanted to quit playing games. Each had gone with someone else, and those relationships had left them empty and disappointed. Why go through all of that again, they agreed. Where had the "get to know each other and be patient" approach gotten them?

Determined not to be disillusioned again, they wanted to tie the knot and got married after knowing each other for only six weeks. "Why the hurry?" people asked. "Why wait?" they replied. The slow deliberate way had hurt them before.

This is called *reacting* instead of acting. Instead of making the best decision for today we muddy the waters by reacting to yesterday.

Sometimes a previous bad decision leads us to make another bad decision. Don't make that mistake when it comes to picking a partner.

How long to wait?

Magic numbers would be nice. Should we wait a quick one month? A respectable three months? How about a reasonable six months? Why not go for a safe year? What is the

HI, I'M LANCE. IF YOU'RE NOT DOING ANYTHING THIS WEEKEND, WOULD YOU LIKE TO GET MARRIED?

scientific formula designed to bring about the best results? If I knew that I would bottle it and sell it at the supermarket.

It might be more helpful to suggest a couple of guidelines and let each person write out her or his own numbers.

1. *Are you over the previous relationship?*

If the hurt is still fresh and the pain is still crippling, it is hard to move on. You need to talk and work out the harm that has been done. You may be asking for trouble by bringing unhealthy emotions into a new relationship.

Tears of joy and tears of sorrow make an odd mixture when it comes to love. Clear out the one before you open the gate to the other.

2. *Do you have a sense that you are settling for a lesser relationship because you lost a better one?*

Do you feel you lost first prize and now you are accepting a kind of booby prize?

This is a sure sign you aren't ready. If the current object of your affection pales by comparison with your former partner, call an end to this now. Any healthy relationship must be based on the fact that you are excited about *this* person.

3. *Do you concentrate more on tomorrow or on yesterday?*

Don't count on a new relationship to heal an old one. Do you find your thoughts fixing on the potential of what is to come, or are you stuck trying to make sense out of what has passed?

How many weeks or months a person should wait depends on other factors. How is the healing process going? Where are attitudes headed? Those questions are more important than checking calendar dates.

Often leads to happiness

Frequently people marry the second or third person they go with. Our spouses are seldom the only people we ever dated. There is no special need to fear a relationship if either person has been involved with someone before.

The issue is "rebounding." Is someone bouncing off another relationship? This implies that the former relationship is not satisfactorily resolved. This could cause sparks later.

Someone who has been happily married for thirty-five or forty years may have "almost" married someone else first.

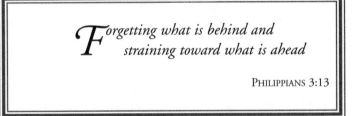

Forgetting what is behind and straining toward what is ahead

PHILIPPIANS 3:13

There may be no need to avoid someone simply because you have been close to someone else.

Paul wasn't discussing marriage when he wrote this but the principle comes in handy:

Getting to know you ♥

1. Do you have a past relationship that still has an emotional grip on you?

2. Has the new person in your life recently severed a relationship?

3. Do you have any feeling that this present relationship is partly rebounding?

4. Are you able to discuss previous relationships?

5. Can you appreciate this new person's strengths and abilities?

CHAPTER 11 ♥

Quick to Forgive

RANDY GREW UP IN A HOME *with parents who withheld forgiveness. They believed children would become spoiled if forgiveness was dished out too freely.*

When Randy broke a plate, his mother scolded him immediately. For weeks she referred to his "clumsiness" in an attempt to drive the lesson home by reminding him of his inadequacies. When company was over she teased Randy about the incident.

Randy learned about forgiveness at home. Unfortunately, he learned to hold it back, forge it into a weapon, and store it for later use. Forgiveness was a tool of destruction, not an instrument for creating beauty.

When Randy marries, he and his wife could face some serious problems related to forgiveness. Will Randy repeat the pattern of his parents or will he learn to distribute forgiveness freely, as God intended?

Background and experience don't totally shape us, but they are big influences. And where deficiencies have occurred, it's important to discuss them and learn new and healthy ways of relating to one another.

Too good to be true

Forgiveness is almost too good to be true. To think that I could insult you, crush your feelings, and an hour later sincerely ask your forgiveness and sincerely receive that pardon is too much to expect. Surely such a thoughtless cretin as I must be made to pay. Suffering should rain down on me for days, weeks, months, or even a year, depending on the seriousness of my offense.

Human reluctance to accept and to give forgiveness in a generous and free manner is a large part of why we stumble over the forgiveness offered by God through Jesus Christ. Experiences with other people have taught us that forgiveness doesn't come easily. To have God hand us total forgiveness with no payment due from us simply blows our minds.

Doesn't God's forgiveness require a waiting period? Isn't there a small price we can pay, like a down payment or a promise to pay later?

How we forgive others depends on how we view God's forgiveness. If we believe God is stingy, mean, halting, and cautious with His pardon, we are likely to treat others the same way.

We are likely to have trouble forgiving others if we have difficulty accepting the generous forgiveness of God. As Ephesians 4:32 states, we are to forgive each other in the same way that God has forgiven us, and that means freely and unconditionally.

How we use unforgiveness

Basketball players don't mind getting fouled because it can work to their advantage. If an opponent hits a player's hand, even accidentally, the offended player gets to shoot a basket while the other team looks on, not allowed to play defense.

Those of us who are slow to forgive enjoy being fouled. When we are hurt or insulted we use the incident to our advantage. We sometimes cannot resist using a friend's mistake to suit our own purposes.

Look at a few passages the Bible uses to describe the absence of forgiveness. See how many apply to you.

1. Nursing a grudge.

John the Baptist condemned Herod for living with Herodius, his brother's wife. Eventually John was beheaded because Herodius nursed a grudge against the apostle and found a way to get revenge against him (see Mark 6:19).

The word *nurse* means to keep alive. Herodius's hate was like a sick patient, and whenever it grew weak or came close to dying, Herodius pumped new life into it. She wasn't about to forgive John and forget the matter.

2. Bearing a grudge.

The Golden Rule that Christ taught comes from the book of Leviticus: "Do not seek revenge or bear a grudge against one of your people, but love your neighbor as yourself. I am the LORD" (19:18).

The word *bear* means to carry or hold up. It seems silly that anyone would waste time and energy carrying anything as useless as a grudge, but many do.

Some of us work hard to hold up our angry grudges where everyone can see what a burden we have to carry. We hold them above our heads like women in Bible times carried pots of water drawn from the village well. And we are eager to allow people to drink the bitter beverage we carry so they will know the reason we are angry. Sadly, all who taste it are poisoned by it.

3. Harboring anger.

God "will not always accuse, nor will he harbor his anger forever" (Psalm 103:9).

Picture a ship sailing swiftly toward a harbor. A storm is coming and the captain doesn't want to lose a precious cargo to the violent sea. What is this precious cargo? Anger. How much wiser if the captain would throw it all overboard and bring the ship safely home.

The captain is like many people who find a safe place to store their anger so nothing can destroy it. Unfortunately, people who store anger have little room for love.

4. Grumbling.

"Don't grumble against each other" (James 5:9).

Grumbling is like distant thunder. You know a storm is coming but you're not sure when it will arrive or how severe it will be.

For days on end grumblers may refuse to discuss why they are angry. They just walk around, sit around, slouch, and mumble under their breath.

This game is called Watch Out—I'm Upset, and it is subtitled, "If you don't figure it out in three guesses, you lose."

The communication is garbled, but there is enough to let everyone know you are ticked.

Grumbling is confusing and nonproductive. A straightforward statement like "Matt, what you did really bugs me" or "Kate, what you said hurt my feelings" is far better than playing mumble, grumble, guess why I'm steamed.

Anger as power

If, for some reason, we consider ourselves inadequate, we will search for ways to make others look inferior. If people we care about hurt us, we might use the offense to make ourselves feel superior.

HONEY, BEFORE YOU COME IN I WANT YOU TO KNOW THAT I FORGIVE YOU FOR STUPIDLY LETTING ME WORK ON THE FURNACE.

It's a sick way to live, but we do it. And we do it against the people we love. We say, "I am angry, so watch out for me. I have power now."

Anger is power, a destructive kind. It's a self-righteous force. Pouting and shouting are the only ways to use this unhealthy force, and when we resort to this form of control we reveal the foul-tempered potentates we have become.

Does any of this sound familiar? Do you see signs of it in yourself or in the person you love?

Loving, mature people will acknowledge the offense, forgive the offender, and throw away the power gained from the offense.

Forgiveness says we would rather have a relationship based on love than on power. Anytime I am given a weapon to use against the person I love, I must break it over one knee and drop it to the ground. Forgiveness enables me to do that.

No relationship can remain healthy if it is based on power. There is no love in force.

If you have lived in a dormitory, you know how easily people can get angry with each other. One of the lessons you may have learned from living with roommates is that you have to forgive and forget quickly if you hope to survive.

Marriage will be more intimate and more intense than any roommate relationship. The possibility of friction is far greater. Consequently, the need for continuous forgiveness.

Don't hold it back. Don't toy with it. Don't even think about using it as a weapon. Instead, give it freely and use it as an instrument to build a beautiful relationship.

How to forgive

When asked if we have forgiven people for wrongs they've done, the answer we often give is, "Well, I think I have." That is neither definite nor satisfying.

Here are some steps to check and see if you have actually forgiven the person.

1. State the offense that needs forgiveness. Be specific.
2. Did you contribute to the mistake?
3. Do you forgive this person now?
4. Can you wish this person well—or do you hold a grudge?
5. Can you take action so this problem is unlikely to happen again?

Forgiveness needs to be an action, if possible. Mere words can leave us feeling empty and confused. By being specific, by accepting any responsibility that is ours, and by wishing offenders well, we can be sure that our forgiveness is real.

Getting to know you ♥

1. As a discussion starter say, "I believe that Jesus Christ has forgiven me for everything I have ever done and for everything I will ever do. How do you feel?" You can help each other measure your concept of forgiveness by discussing the forgiveness and freedom you have found in Christ.

2. Is either of you nursing old grudges to keep them alive—against friends? parents? siblings? the church? God? When will you be willing to let them go? now?

CHAPTER 12

Guidelines for Sex

THE QUESTION OF WHEN to have sex bothers almost every young adult. Generally, there is a gulf of five to ten or fifteen years between the onset of puberty and marriage.

That's a terribly long time to wait for relief from sexual pressure. It doesn't take long before the temptations are almost unmanageable. The simplistic solutions offered by some advisors range from ridiculous to impractical:

Take long walks.

Take cold showers.

Get a hobby.

Stay away from the opposite sex.

The truth is, there are no easy ways to control sexual desire. Waiting until marriage is tough, Tough, TOUGH!

Anything worth having . . .

You're no fool. You know what's coming next. Anything worth having is worth waiting for. Parents have used this line for generations to teach children the value of everything from bicycles to piercing ears. Unfortunately, this teaching has lost popularity during the last couple of decades and waiting is no longer considered of value.

But trite as it sounds, it is still true. Perhaps a better, more convincing way to say it is: Anything you have to wait for will have more value to you. Those who have sex with the first (or any) available person will eventually come to consider sex cheap.

SERIOUS? OF COURSE IT'S SERIOUS! WE'VE DATED EACH OTHER FOR A WHOLE WEEK NOW.

An economic principle called the law of supply and demand explains the concept well. If there is a big supply of something, the price for it drops. In other words, it has less value. We see this in everything from the job market to works of art. If you have a necessary skill that no one else can perform, you can name your salary. But if everyone can learn to do what you do, you're probably going to receive only minimum wage for your service. Similarly, if Leonardo da Vinci had mass-produced the *Mona Lisa*, it wouldn't have the value it has today as one of a kind.

So it's a law of human nature. We value what is rare and devalue what is commonplace. For sex to remain valuable you can't allow it to become commonplace.

I know of no easy way to keep this from happening. But I do have some guidelines that might help you keep sex valuable in your own life so that in marriage your sexual relationship will be as gratifying as possible.

1. Don't get married for sex.

Sex can be on your list of reasons for getting married, but it shouldn't be at the top. Make sure you have at least nine other good reasons for getting married.

For young couples, sex rages like white-water rapids. Like a raging river, however, the degree of sexual tumult depends on the season. This may be difficult for young people to believe, but sexual desire doesn't rage all the time. Other characteristics, therefore, are necessary to keep a relationship from becoming stagnant when the waters are calm.

Sex is a natural and major force in wanting to get married. God planned it this way. He created a system that makes us desire each other. There is nothing wrong with His plan, but

> *For this reason a man will leave his father and mother and be united to his wife, and they will become one flesh.*
>
> GENESIS 2:24

desire is only the beginning and the easiest part of it.

Life offers few pleasures as great as married love, but too often we confuse sexual pleasure for love and make sex our primary goal.

Young people at the height of sexual tension want to consummate a relationship with the person they feel so passionately about. "How can it be wrong when it feels so right?" a popular song once asked. The answer is, "Easily." Many, many things that seem right in a moment of passion are seen as incredibly stupid and wrong the next morning or the next week or the next year.

2. Don't marry without a desire for sex.

Suppose you like to discuss the French language, oriental cooking, the Minor Prophets, and Mongolian art, but you aren't attracted physically. Will mental stimulation be enough to hold your relationship together?

Probably not.

More than likely, one of you will begin to feel sorry for yourself. You will know something is missing. Resentment will soon follow and trouble will be close on its heels.

If you have no interest in making love, you need to ask some serious questions. Why does the physical vacuum exist? Will the lack of drive for each other cause problems later? How can you know for sure?

Platonic attractions usually make shaky marriages, but I have met couples who have been happily married for twenty years with little or no physical relationship. This can and does happen, but I would not recommend that you risk marrying if no sexual attraction exists between you.

3. Don't marry because you already had sex.

If you made a mistake in ordering airline tickets, would you live for the next fifty years in Nome when you were planning to relocate to Rome? If you hate cold weather it wouldn't make much sense to move to Nome. Nor does it make sense to marry a person because you made a mistake and had sex. Sex before marriage is wrong, but it is not a lifelong commitment. And marriage will not undo the wrong, it will only compound it.

But, someone objects, isn't sex the same as being married? No. Absolutely not. No one in our society is married without intending to be. Marriage can't be accidental. It is a willful act.

True, God's plan is that two people are to become "one flesh" in marriage. But becoming one in marriage is much more than a sexual act. Those who have sex with a number of people certainly are not married to them all!

Never fall prey to this reasoning: "You have to marry me now; we've already had sex." That's pure manipulation and should be recognized as such.

4. Ask forgiveness for sinful sexual encounters.

Guilt is a trap. It clamps shut with a force that can hold us forever. Only Christ can free us. One of His most outstanding gifts is the freedom of forgiveness, which we can receive because He paid the sacrifice for our sins.

None of us need enter a relationship still trapped by guilt or regret for sinful sexual encounters. Whatever we have done

> *In whom we have redemption, the forgiveness of sins.*
>
> COLOSSIANS 1:14

can be forgiven and erased. Christians can set things straight with their partners and receive cleansing. Rather than live in the shadow of our sin, we can live in the light of God's pardon.

What bothers you? Don't let it spoil your relationship. Tell God about it. Tell each other about it if necessary. Take the load off and be free to enjoy the fullness of your future.

The saddest couples are frequently the ones who are haunted, who feel the past creeping up on them. Christ offers us a better future than this.

5. Make sex the best it can be.

Sex has a place and a purpose. Its place is marriage and its purpose is to express full and total love. Every other place and reason for having sex is dangerous and unfulfilling. Although sex produces children, procreation is not its main function.

The Bible pays this tribute to married sex: "Marriage should be honored by all, and the marriage bed kept pure, for God will judge the adulterer and all the sexually immoral" (Hebrews 13:4).

Married sex is blessed and protected by God. All other sexual relationships are outside God's original intention and therefore are subject to much grief and pain.

It's tough to hold the standard, but millions of people are very happy they did.

6. Refuse to believe the myths.

Myth: *Practice makes perfect*

This argument keeps sprouting up like crabgrass. How can you know if you are sexually compatible unless you try it first? This is a nearsighted argument and most people who use it do so to get what they want.

When two people love each other, they almost always become sexually compatible. At least 99 out of 100 couples reach compatibility in a short time. The other 1 percent may need some instruction, but this is almost never the case. The facts are:

- There is nothing you can learn about sex before marriage that you could not learn after the wedding.
- There are no adjustments that can be made before a marriage that cannot be made after the wedding.
- Any fears about sex can be relieved either by some simple information before the wedding or by careful practice during the marriage.

Sex before marriage can result in much guilt and regret and many complications, while providing no lasting benefits for the marriage itself.

Myth: *If we're sexually compatible, we can work out our other differences.*

Don't kid yourself into thinking that sex is an iron that can smooth out all the wrinkles in a relationship. Unless you use it correctly, it will burn holes in the fabric of your love.

Myth: *Everyone does it.*

Don't be persuaded by this old argument. Everybody does not do it. A lot of people still wait. You aren't the last, sole holdout dying in the heat of sexual passion. Plenty of people wait; you just don't hear about them.

Myth: *If we really love each other we should show it.*

Never, never, never fall for the old line, "If you really loved me . . . ." This dusty, whining plea is still around and, incredibly, still working.

Turn the constant begging and groping for sex into a helpful discussion of patience, tolerance, and caring.

7. Expect respect.

If you have been going together for a while the pressure to have sex is surely mounting. Your mind has a hard time controlling your body when it's screaming for attention. You believe sex outside marriage is wrong, but the pressure to give in is wearing you down.

Hang in there. You have every right to expect respect for your physical, spiritual, and mental well-being. If you compromise what you believe, you will hurt not only yourself, but also your partner and your relationship.

If one demands sex, despite the other's moral values, take a step back and reevaluate your relationship. Does one of you want sex so desperately that he or she is willing to belittle and damage the other person's conscience for a few minutes of pleasure and relief?

Explain the situation in those terms. It may cause disappointment, confusion, and pouting. But if your sweetheart continues to ask you to go against your conscience, she or he may simply be trying to use you for selfish gratification.

If you split up over this matter your heart will be broken and you will carry the pain for a long time. You want a relationship built on respect not on manipulation.

8. Fall in love with a person not a body.

I continually meet people who got married because they were dying to get in bed together. As the excitement of sex tapered off, the two discovered they had little else in common.

Find a person you can love and you won't have trouble making love to the body. If you find a body to love, you could wake up to discover that you have nothing in common with the person.

In one of Scripture's more sensuous passages the author pays a salute to good physical love in a married context:

Married sex can fulfill all of its promises for those who show patience. Sex in marriage is so enjoyable, so personal, so fulfilling, and so satisfying that it is well worth the difficult years of restraint and sexual frustration.

> *A loving doe, a graceful deer—*
> *may her breasts satisfy you always,*
> *may you ever be captivated by her love.*
>
> PROVERBS 5:19

Getting to know you ♥

1. How would you describe the sexual attraction between the two of you? What does this tell you about your relationship?

2. What can you do to lower the temptation to have sex too soon?

3. Besides physical attraction, what other major interests do you have in common?

4. Is one of you pressuring the other to have sex? Discuss the consequences of pressuring someone (even in manipulative, subtle ways) to do something he or she believes is wrong.

CHAPTER 13 ♥

One in the Spirit

ALICE ALWAYS DREAMED *of marrying a Christian so the two of them could become youth sponsors in a local church. Her mental image was perfectly clear. She pictured herself and her husband leading a group of teenagers in a lively discussion of Christ and commitment.*

Whenever Alice mentioned her plan to Joe he would smile and grunt, "Sure." Within six months of marriage, Alice was sitting at home with her new husband watching reruns of Seinfeld. *Exhausted after a day's work, Joe wasn't about to spend his time with a bunch of screaming young people. Too late, Alice discovered how he really felt about it. Wanting so much to believe that he shared her vision, she failed to probe beneath the surface of his words.*

Our spouses are the greatest human influence on our spiritual lives. They have the unique ability to motivate us to new heights or drag us down to spiritual despair. Just as often, partners keep us in the mediocre middle. Without passion to serve God couples frequently stay in spiritual limbo.

Since the effect is enormous, thinking Christians will stop and ask, "If I marry this person, how will my personal faith be swayed?"

Faith isn't like kitchen linoleum. Couples can compromise about floor covering to keep each other reasonably happy. But religious convictions are not easily adjusted. When one partner feels a call to discipleship and the other is a Christmas Christian, both will be uncomfortable.

No spiritual guarantees

None of us can say how the fire inside our souls might burn two years from now. A halfhearted, nominal Christian could become a spiritual leader far beyond anyone's expectations. And today's disciple can also become tomorrow's dropout.

Every one of us must take responsibility for her or his own faithfulness to God. No one else can hold it together for you or for me.

Nevertheless, we must try our best to select spiritually compatible mates because we know what a tremendous influence we will have on each other.

Having done that, we try to grow together as Christians rather than drift apart. Openness and honesty are the best methods to make that happen.

The questions you ask each other should be deeper than "Which worship service do you like best, 9:30 or 11:00?"

If possible, get into a study group. The opportunity to share with others can be eye-opening for both of you.

No litmus test

A litmus test measures a single factor, and there is no single test to determine spiritual compatibility. Would that life could be so simple. Despite this, people are always coming up with supposedly surefire tests. We hear things like:

- The real test is whether or not you can pray together.
- Never marry anyone who doesn't go to Sunday school.
- Ask him when he gave his life totally to Christ.
- How does she feel about tithing?
- Did he go to a Christian school?

Since we are living, dynamic individuals, there is a great deal to consider that is not observable in a few months or even a few years of dating. Without discussion there will be no understanding or agreement.

Although there is no reliable test, there are some thoughtful questions that will give you some fairly reliable clues. They are designed to provoke discussion and understanding, not argument and disagreement. Nor is this a quiz to see if you can both pass Bible 101. The questions furnish enough material for a few evenings of discussion to help you get to know the person you might spend the rest of your life with.

1. Are you both Christians?

Don't worry that you may not say the right words, and don't be afraid to express doubts or fears. Don't correct each other or look shocked at unusual answers. The major thing you need to find out is what each of you believes about Jesus Christ. For Christians, Christ is the major issue.

Don't start nitpicking and get into arguments about issues Christians have disagreed about for centuries, like eternal security and eschatology. And don't get all tied up in knots over whether or not Christ could sin or whether He would vote Republican or Democrat.

Don't stumble over word choices. Many of us listen for pet phrases and in doing so we make words instead of belief and action the criteria for agreement.

Take time to reach beyond mere words. Who is Christ to you? What does He mean in your life? Do you trust Him for eternal life? Are your sins forgiven?

This can be a growing experience for both of you. You will probably show each other a new dimension of faith.

If one of you is not a Christian and has no desire to become one, slow down, back off, and reconsider your relationship.

When a Christian and a non-Christian marry each other, they start with a problem no one wants: misunderstanding. They will be unable to share the most important part of their lives with the person who is supposed to be an intimate, loving partner. They will be trying to mix water and oil.

The non-Christian may be a fantastic person. Generous, thoughtful, loving, honest. But there is a barrier, and it is no small obstacle. To marry such a person means you will never share your personal faith in God. For the believer this is an unreasonable restraint.

The Bible gives a sweeping principle. Believers and nonbelievers should not be tied together.

If you attach two cars by their rear bumpers, only one of them can move forward. That is what happens when two people going in opposite directions unite themselves in marriage. The stronger one goes forward, pulling the weaker one along backward. If the two are of equal strength, they will pull

> *D*o not be yoked together with unbelievers.
> *For what do righteousness and wickedness have in common? Or what fellowship can light have with darkness?*
>
> 2 CORINTHIANS 6:14

until one or both bumpers come off. Neither car will reach its destination intact.

You don't have to look very far to find unhappy people who married non-Christians. They ache to share their faith and to express it alongside the person they love.

2. What shade of Christian?

We would like to think that a Christian is a Christian is a Christian, but this is a complex world and Christians disagree about a lot of things, some of which may be important to you.

Christians can marry assuming that they are in perfect agreement about religious matters and later have problems they never anticipated. Discuss these questions and any others that might occur to you:

- Will the vows say "obey"?
- What are the male and what are the female roles?
- Where will you go to church?
- What does submission mean?

- How do you feel about birth control?
- Will your infants be baptized?
- Will the children take communion?

These may seem like harmless subjects, but each is a potential battleground.

3. How much involvement?

The discussion of personal faith is no doctrinal exam. There is more to believing than agreeing on how many angels can sit on the head of a pin or which person of the Trinity is

DO I TAKE THIS TO MEAN YOU DON'T SHARE THE SAME VISION I HAVE FOR A HOSPITALITY MINISTRY, HONEY?

responsible for answering prayer. If one partner is interested in actively serving God while the other wants only to salute the heavenly Father in passing, those two lovers have something to work out.

Seldom do two people serve at the same pace. One may want to sing, teach, organize, and even march while the other would rather dabble at helping the needy on rare occasions.

Talk about differences. You may not reach agreement on every subject, but at least you will find out what burns inside. Your individual passion to serve God will have a heavy influence on how compatible you will be.

Churches are filled with spiritual widows and widowers. They have spiritually dead spouses who care nothing about worship or church involvement.

Beyond any question of right or wrong is the need for harmony. The goal isn't to find someone who is identical, but we each need a person whose passion for service to God is compatible with our own. Don't let another friend or even a book tell you if you are a "good" couple or not. Only you know that. Questions about spirituality will help the two of you understand each other and yourselves.

Getting to know you ♥

The following are word associations. Take time to respond to each word or phrase. Go over them slowly and see how much they mean to you. Remember, this is not a test. No one passes or fails.

1. *Baptism*
   What is its purpose?

At what age or stage should someone be baptized?
What method do you prefer? Why?

2. *Communion*
   Why do we take communion?
   Who should take it?
   How often?

3. *Church services*
   Do you prefer guitars or organs?
   Do you like liturgical or nonliturgical?
   How much responsive reading?
   What kind of music do you appreciate?

4. *Church emphasis*
   Evangelism?
   Teaching?
   Inspirational?
   Personal help?
   Sharing?

5. *Fellowship*
   Small groups?
   Mixing among the congregation?
   Socials?
   Classes?
   Ball teams?

6. *Church size*
   Large?
   Medium?
   Small?

7. *Attendance*

Holidays?
Monthly?
Weekly?
Two or three times a week?
More?

8. *Christian service*

Attendance at church only?
Help teach youth, children, or adults?
Help underprivileged?
Clean church?
Usher, sing in choir, or other?

9. *Personal commitment*

Daily Bible reading?
Couple Bible reading?
Individual Bible reading?
As you want to?

10. Other

What other subjects would you like to discuss? Add whatever you think is pertinent.

These categories are not of equal importance. Individuals and couples must decide what they can live with enthusiastically.

CHAPTER 14 ♥

Maturity Makes a Difference

DEBBIE HAD GREAT NEWS. *From the look on her face her parents knew it was something terrific.*

"I've met a guy," she said. "You're really going to like him. He isn't perfect, but when you consider him as a total package he's really fantastic. I guess I must finally be growing up. I didn't have to find the perfect one."

No doubt Debbie is growing up, and because of that she and Doug have the prospects for a wonderful relationship.

An old adage says that marriage is only for adults. Unfortunately a large number of children end up at altars reciting vows. They may be adults in age, but they are still children emotionally. And if they cannot mature quickly enough, their marriages will last about as long as two children dressing up in their parents' clothes and playing house.

Maturity sounds terribly boring. We picture people with matted gray hair who walk their dogs and worry about Social Security. That's a gross misunderstanding of the word. Maturity has nothing to do with age or personality. It has everything to do with attitude toward life.

Mature people laugh, have fun, are adventurous, creative, energetic, and curious. They sparkle when they tell stories and they enjoy personal accomplishment.

But mature people do not laugh at other people or have fun at someone else's expense. They do not value thrills above the safety of their loved ones. Their creative expressions are not crude or unkind. They understand the value of sitting still and thinking before making decisions. They tell stories to entertain and instruct, not to ridicule. And their personal goals are not reached by climbing over other people. In other words, they are responsible, caring, dependable, dedicated, and unselfish.

The Bible is concerned about maturity and how it behaves. Let's look at what the Scriptures consider reasonable development and see how it applies to the special person in your life.

Mature people act sensibly

This doesn't mean we should look for partners who are stuffy and sullen. Acting sensibly doesn't mean we are always predictable and unimaginative in our behavior. Mature people are childlike, but not childish.

Childish people pout, demand their own way, lose their tempers, break things, throw fits, and toss food around the room. No sensible person is eager to marry someone like that.

"*I had no life at all,*" *Tricia said. "Todd demanded that I come straight home and do what he wanted. If I didn't he shouted, slammed doors, made threats. He was always throwing fits."*

Her husband had the maturity of a three-year-old. He had not put childish things behind him.

In contrast, a childlike partner can camp in the park, explore mountains, play games, and laugh late into the night. A childlike mate isn't afraid to enjoy life and would love to enjoy life with you.

Childlike behavior is mature; childish behavior is immature, and the apostle Paul put that behavior away (*Learning from Children,* Paul Welter, Tyndale House, 1984).

> *When I was a child, I thought like a child, I reasoned like a child. When I became a man, I put childish things behind me.*
>
> 1 CORINTHIANS 13:11

Mature people are growing

Don't wait for the perfectly mature partner. Cobwebs will form in your hair and dust balls will fill your ears before that prince or that princess comes along. What you want is someone moving toward maturity, someone who sees its value, who wants to achieve it.

Some Christians in the city of Philippi had a short supply of maturity. Paul didn't tell them to drop dead, get out, or disappear. He simply said that God would continue to work with anyone who was not mature enough to see things correctly (see Philippians 3:15).

If one of you is not yet mature, you don't necessarily have to abandon the relationship. Look for growth. Encourage it without nagging. Look for willingness to learn and develop.

Never reject clay because it is not a great statue. Look for its potential. Has it hardened into a permanently ugly lump, or is it still pliable? Is it still being molded by the Heavenly Potter?

When Pat and I got married, I knew nothing about how to treat a woman or how to share with a partner. I was only semi-

WHAT DO YOU THINK? ARE WE MATURE
ENOUGH TO GET MARRIED?

civilized. But Pat didn't give up on me after two weeks or after two years. She saw potential in me and encouraged me to reach it.

Growth and movement are signs that maturity can actually happen. Stubbornness and intransigence are signs of hopelessness and death.

Mature people know the difference between good and evil.

Jackie had the qualities everyone wants: Looks, character, talent, spirit, thoughtfulness—the whole ball of wax. Unfortunately, she melted when she got too close to someone who knew how to heat up a relationship. Ignoring the advice of family and friends, Jackie married Paul. He treated her well. He bought her gifts, took her out to nice places, and truly enjoyed her company. Paul knew how to be romantic—but that was all he knew.

When he realized he couldn't afford the romantic lifestyle, his darker side began to dominate. Late one evening Jackie got a call from the police. They had caught her husband robbing a grocery store with a gun in his hand.

How did a smart woman like Jackie get mixed up with a man who didn't know the difference between good and evil? No one wants to blame her, but we should ask ourselves where her decision-making process went awry. What should she have looked for, what should she have asked to find out if Paul knew the difference between right and wrong?

Signs of maturity

- Mature people do not try to hurt their partners.
- They do not use a spouse for personal satisfaction.

- They do not behave in ways that put others in danger.
- They do not lie.
- They do not ignore their partners' needs.
- They do not put their needs above everyone else's.

So what do mature people do?

- Mature people try to protect their mates from pain.
- Mature people accept their mates as partners.
- They look for ways to be helpful.
- They call and keep in touch when they are away.
- They express warm feelings.
- They practice unselfishness.
- They value truth.
- They protect their loved ones.

All of us have moments of pure evil. We say things we wish we had swallowed. We do things that are cheap and inconsiderate.

But mature people do not live that way. They know the difference between right and wrong, and they pursue the right.

Mature people show some wisdom

No one wants to marry a fool—yet many do. They hook up with partners who lack good sense. One of the richest commodities any person possesses is a healthy supply of wisdom or plain, old-fashioned good sense.

To have wisdom, you don't have to be a gray-bearded philosopher. You just have to be fair, caring, even-handed, able to see the whole picture, self-controlled, and considerate.

A wise person does not think like the average person. The "wisdom" of this age promotes trial marriages, easy divorce, selfish goals, and shallow commitment. These do not show the good sense you expect to find in mature people.

Never apologize for expecting a wise partner. And make sure the terms *carefree* and *fun-loving* are not euphemisms for *irresponsible* and *immature*.

Mature people stick it out

All of us cut our losses and pull out sometimes. That doesn't make us unfit. But if we develop a pattern of pulling out, trouble is lurking.

> *We do, however, speak a message of wisdom among the mature, but not the wisdom of this age or of the rulers of this age, who are coming to nothing.*
>
> 1 CORINTHIANS 2:6

Patterns are hard to identify in young people, but there are a few clues to look for.

- Does one of you continually drop classes?
- Do you fail to keep financial commitments?
- Are you often late for work?
- Do you switch jobs frequently?
- When you disagree, does one of you run and hide to avoid confrontation?
- Do you treat friends with callous indifference?
- Do you break dates without calling?
- Do you break dates frequently?

Add to the list whatever else you think is important. Look for a pattern and ask yourself what it means.

Maybe you are maturing slowly and eventually will make the ideal marriage partner. But don't bet on it.

If a cut-and-run pattern is obvious in either of you, discuss it. If you are mature enough to marry, you should be able to demonstrate commitment, not just talk about it.

Before you laugh this point off, think about Heidi. You probably know at least one person like her.

Heidi has a small child and is pregnant. Her husband of three years has moved to another state. He is supposed to pay child support, but she's lucky to get a payment every other month, and often it's not for the full amount.

She and her child live below the poverty level in a small, sparsely furnished apartment. She remembers the signs of cut-and-run her husband showed before they married. Whenever they had a disagreement, he would go off with his friends and not call for a month or two. She thought a family would help him settle down, but she was wrong.

Now think about another woman.

One month before Amanda's wedding forty years ago a doctor told her she had a crippling disease. When her fiancé heard the report, he insisted that they go on with the marriage because he loved her deeply.

Now they have three grown children and are as happy as otters on a riverbank.

The book of James tells us that trials test our faith and that this testing results in perseverance—the ability to stick it out through thick or thin, or as the marriage vows say, in sickness or in health, in poverty or in wealth.

Mature people come in all varieties. Some wear funny hats, scream at ball games, order pizza at 1:00 A.M. But most importantly, mature partners are dedicated to making a great marriage no matter how difficult it may be.

We can either run away from difficulties or grow stronger and wiser because of them. Which habit are you developing?

> *Perseverance must finish its work so that you may be mature and complete, not lacking anything.*
>
> JAMES 1:4

Getting to know you ♥

1. On a scale of 1 to 10, rate your own and each other's maturity levels.

2. Recall and discuss an act or an attitude of maturity you each have observed in the other.

3. Discuss signs of increased maturity you have seen in each other since you started dating.

CHAPTER 15 ♥

Cash, Credit Cards, Collateral

ONE SERIOUS CLASH almost all couples have is money. Every group of couples I have asked has put this problem near the top. Money, for all its positive potential, is like gunpowder ready to blow up at the smallest spark.

The answer to the money problem seems simple. Make enough so there isn't any reason to fight about it. Then both of you can buy what you want.

Mark that answer wrong. The war over finances has almost nothing to do with how much money a couple has. Poor, middle-class, and rich people all have friction over finances. The real problem lies in different attitudes toward money, not in how much you have stashed in the closet.

When Jodie got married, handling money was a new concept to her. Her parents never wanted her to worry about finances so they never discussed the subject in her presence. For twenty years they never talked about bills, savings accounts, credit cards, or even paychecks. Although Jodie wasn't able to have everything she wanted, her parents never explained why. She had no introduction to the practical world of making ends meet.

After six months of marriage, Jodie had gotten her and her husband's bank account into total chaos. They had no idea how much money they had, whom they owed or how much, and what they had already paid.

To Jodie, money was something that simply floated in and floated out. She couldn't imagine how anyone could control this elusive green and plastic stuff.

On the opposite end of the spectrum was Joyce.

Joyce's attitude toward money confused Kevin the whole time they dated. She considered every dollar as an investment. She squirreled each spare dime into bonds, stocks, real estate, or whatever she saw as long term, refusing to spend any on herself.

Slowly a light went on in Kevin's head and he realized that Joyce had no concept of the present. All of her financial perception was focused on the future. Joyce was obsessed with a distant goal that prevented her from enjoying the here and now.

Kevin wasn't sure he wanted to live only for this foggy future so he slowly distanced himself from the extremely cautious Joyce.

Few people are sure how they feel about money, but a few open-ended questions could help them find out. A great discussion starter is: "How do your parents handle their finances?"

That question can lead almost anywhere. Do they have credit cards? Can either of them write checks or does only one person take care of that? If both work, do they keep their money separate or together? Do they buy appliances on credit? Do they have savings?

This isn't a time for interrogation; it's a time for honest questions.

Let those questions lead to the next natural one: "How do you feel about that arrangement?"

Expect anything from warm approval to a red-faced denunciation of the family financial system. Now the two of you are talking and you are finding out more about yourselves.

Money guidelines

Fortunately the Bible gives us some excellent criteria to use in handling finances. It won't tell us whether or not to buy a video camera, but it will help us put money in its proper perspective. This becomes a great starting point for a helpful conversation.

Beware of money lovers.

Many of us walk a wobbly line. One moment we want only enough money to lead comfortable lives; the next moment we want to gobble up as much cash as possible, and the next we are convinced to give it all away. Money is an experienced tempter that lures us into all kinds of deadly traps and mercilessly murders our moral values.

We have to worry about people for whom finances are the center of existence. Their educations, career choices, friends, leisure time, and spiritual goals revolve around getting and keeping wealth.

Although they may deny that this is true, their attitudes and actions reveal that the meaning of life is money. All their time, energy, and creativity are used to find ways to make more green stuff.

The Bible's basic warning goes like this: "The love of money is a root of all kinds of evil. Some people, eager for money, have wandered from the faith and pierced themselves with many griefs" (1 Timothy 6:10).

There is nothing wrong with having financial goals and planning for a secure future. But there is something desperately wrong if wealth is the primary motivation in a person's life.

Many believe that success and money are synonymous. As Christians, however, we should have a far broader concept of success. Faith, service, caring, and healthy

OKAY, SHOW ME WHERE IT SAYS,
"THOU SHALT NOT BUY A CAMCORDER."

relationships are just a few of the things that characterize true success. The accumulation of wealth is a low priority in the Christian system.

Money is an insatiable dictator. We can never do enough to please it.

A young woman I know grew up without a father and her family had little money when she was a child. Today she and her husband work feverishly for every dollar they can collect. Her idea of happiness is to have two jobs and a husband who works the same.

She intensely dislikes church because the preacher talks about money. She is worried that the church is after her cash.

> *Whoever loves money never has money enough; whoever loves wealth is never satisfied with his income.*
> *This too is meaningless.*
>
> ECCLESIASTES 5:10

Money has become her god and she worships it tirelessly. Christ taught that we cannot love both God and the wealth of this world (see Matthew 6:24).

Beware of debt

Our society is built on the shaky foundation of debt. We make car and house payments most of our lives and often develop an addiction to credit cards, installment loans, and other buy now/pay later plans.

The Bible doesn't forbid debt but it does give some severe warnings about it.

- Don't accept the responsibility for someone else's debt (Proverbs 6:1; 22:26).
- Don't let debts go unpaid (Romans 13:7–8).
- It is wicked to borrow and not repay (Psalm 37:21).
- The borrower is servant to the lender (Proverbs 22:7).

There are two types of debt: serviceable debt (or manageable debt) and runaway debt. Too often a couple's financial condition escalates from the convenience of the first to the misery of the second.

Many people who found they could not control the allure of instant credit have had the good sense to take a pair of scissors to the plastic monsters.

Beware of dishonesty

Chad is a schemer. He is always working on a special deal that is just a tad shady. He wants to make it big, and his conscience doesn't care how he does it. So every plan he conceives is less than honest.

The LORD abhors dishonest scales, but accurate weights are his delight.

PROVERBS 11:1

Chad knows how to make products seem better than they really are, and he has developed sales pitches that cover up some of the facts. In a word, he is a shyster.

He makes a decent living, but he's been really irritable lately. He's starting to worry that some of his deals have gone beyond deceitful to illegal. He's not sure, but he thinks a couple of them might even have been fraudulent. If so, he could go to jail and lose everything. He doesn't know what to do. He would start being honest if he could, but an honest living won't pay all his bills.

People like Chad are more common than you might think. They live in constant tension because their greed started flirting with deception and finally gave in to its charms.

When you love someone, it's easy to overlook questionable ethics. But in the long run the lack of financial integrity brings a great deal of pain.

An emphasis on giving

Generosity shows strength of character. It doesn't come naturally to everyone but can be learned and cultivated. The opposite of a generous spirit is one that is self-centered and stingy. People with this type of attitude tend to be unpleasant because they have trouble giving of themselves or of anything they possess.

> *A generous man will prosper; he who refreshes others will himself be refreshed.*
>
> PROVERBS 11:25

People in love are at their most generous. If someone claims to love you and yet is stingy, you have every reason to question that love. Furthermore, there is little chance of people becoming generous to others if they are stingy with the ones they care for the most.

What does it say if the person you go with is always trying to beat you out of a dollar? No one needs a partner who shows love with lavish gifts, but a miser is no gem either.

Extravagant and foolish giving can be a problem, but quarter-clutchers are no fun at all.

An emphasis on saving

Ants are creatures of little strength, yet they store up their food in the summer.

PROVERBS 30:25

Smart people live for today and tomorrow. The value of saving is difficult for many young people to comprehend. They are more interested in the present. Frankly, that's a refreshing contrast to those who pile up all their goods and live only for a tomorrow that may not come. But neither extreme is healthy.

If your sweetheart has never saved a dime, plant a few seeds of suggestion. Don't expect a harvest too soon, but if the concept takes root you could have a decent future together.

Money to finance tomorrow's dreams, as a buffer in case of emergency, for recreation—these are all reasons to save.

Young people enjoy talking about where they want to live and in what kind of house or apartment. They even dream about children and nurseries.

Saving is what helps make our dreams come true.

Getting to know you ♥

1. What does money mean to you? Pick out three words from the following list that best describe why you want money. Make your choices individually and then discuss them. This isn't a pass/fail quiz. The two of you may arrive at totally different answers and become a fantastic couple.

security	*generosity*	*food*
savings	*prestige*	*freedom*
spending	*investment*	*children*
fun	*travel*	*cars*
power	*clothing*	*stewardship*
influence	*home*	*frugal*

Explain to each other the reasons for your selections. What is there in your personality or background or concept of the future that made you lean this way? And precisely what do you mean by the words you picked out?

Don't be surprised if one of you has given the subject hardly any thought. Most young people don't crystalize their thoughts about money until they start their careers and realize how costly it is just to live.

2. Another way to get in touch with attitudes about money is to play this game: If you received a thousand dollars—

no strings attached—what would you do with it? Again, don't look for right or wrong answers. Just answer the question and then discuss your answers.

CHAPTER 16 ♥

The Volcano Watch

RACHEL KNEW FOSTER BLEW UP *more than most people. He frequently slammed car doors, room doors, and cabinet doors. When things didn't go his way, Foster yelled and sometimes became verbally abusive. Once he pushed Rachel onto the couch and stomped out of the house.*

Through all of his tantrums Rachel rationalized that Foster was under a great deal of pressure. He had trouble with his mother. He didn't eat right. Rachel convinced herself that Foster's condition was temporary and that love and marriage would mellow him.

Most of Rachel's friends didn't say anything; they simply stayed away "to give them space." Her sister mentioned Foster's problem once but Rachel became defensive.

After marriage their frustrations increased and Foster's temper fits became more frequent. A couple of times he hit his wife.

Rachel ignored an important principle: A hot-tempered person will burn whoever gets close.

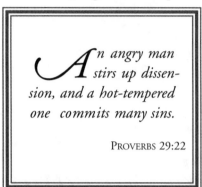

An angry man stirs up dissension, and a hot-tempered one commits many sins.

PROVERBS 29:22

Hot-tempered and noisy are not the same. People may express themselves with great gusts of wind and exaggerated gestures without being angry or out of control. They may simply have learned a boisterous way of communication. They are willing to tone down when they realize they are being misunderstood.

Handled correctly, these people are grateful when someone helps them acquire greater social skills. Nothing wrong with that.

A hot-tempered person is another variety.

The verge of violence

When Joe tries to communicate, he's always on the border of violence. His verbal and body language are clear forms of intimidation. By using extreme behavior he tells everyone to watch out or risk getting hurt.

People like Joe are usually worse in their own homes. They see family members as personal possessions and think they have a right to growl and stalk and punish anyone or anything inside their own walls. A few even believe they are obligated to be mean.

I don't want to sensationalize this problem, but it is only a few short steps from bad temper to violence and physical abuse. Outrageous behavior should not be taken lightly.

Actual violence

There is more spouse and child abuse than statistics indicate. A great many people are getting knocked around. Many are maimed. More than a few are killed.

One of the saddest sights I have seen on the news was a parent of a married daughter who had been murdered. The mother said, "We all knew he was bad news, but she wouldn't listen."

TEMPER? WHO'S GOT A TEMPER?

If more than one person has expressed concern over your relationship because one of you has a bad temper, get counseling immediately. Make an appointment with someone qualified to work with you on this problem. If either of you is unwilling to do this, there is little hope that your relationship can be salvaged.

I have counseled many spouses who were married to violent partners and didn't know what to do. As Christians they were reluctant to divorce, but they lived in constant fear. No person should even get close to such an explosive situation.

No easy solution

Those who use anger and violence to communicate and control people didn't start last Tuesday. They didn't one day discover that the *National Geographic* subscription had lapsed and begin tossing chairs around the living room.

More than likely they have used this approach to problem-solving for years. They may have learned this behavior from parents. Some developed this habit as a disguise for feelings of weakness. And a number may suffer from a chemical imbalance.

One thing we can say with authority: few of the cases will have a simple solution.

Young people in love want to help each other, and a few can. But normally those involved in a relationship are too emotionally involved to think this through clearly. Idealism, passion, and love all muddy the waters.

Angry people have learned how effective verbal and physical violence can be. Therefore, an offer to help them is positive reinforcement of their negative behavior. The more they win through intimidation, the more often they will use it. Attacks will increase in frequency and intensity.

Let someone else prescribe a cure—someone who is firm, experienced, and objective. Don't let your heart put your body and soul at risk.

One estimate says that 10 children die every day from child abuse. That's 3,650 a year. Most are victims of parents who had problems with their temper and didn't control themselves.

Calm people

People who control themselves don't make the headlines, but they make much better partners than those who rant and rave and break things.

Who do you know who is married to a strong, confident person? Who has a husband who doesn't have to prove he is a man by using his fists? Who has a wife who can stand on her own two feet without using intimidation? Partners like that are available. And they are worth waiting for.

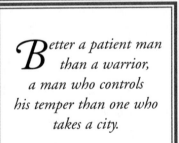

Better a patient man than a warrior, a man who controls his temper than one who takes a city.

PROVERBS 16:32

What's the big deal?

Many who read this chapter will wonder what's the big deal. They have never seen or experienced violence and never expect to. Fantastic! It would be great if these warnings applied to no one. But millions who have turned a blind eye to this subject have later regretted it.

Even people supposed to be Christians are out there hitting each other and covering up the problem. Wives and husbands lie about the bruises on their arms and faces.

There is no justification for any type of abuse. If the person you are dating has hit you in anger, call off the relationship immediately! Don't sympathize. Don't rationalize. Don't play psychologist and look for ways to help. Say goodbye! When violent people receive a response to their physical abuse, they are encouraged, not discouraged. If they see people afraid, compliant, or even fighting back, their violence has gotten a response and therefore is perceived as working.

Since people are generally on their best behavior in dating relationships, if they become physically abusive then, you don't want to be around to find out how their behavior will degenerate after marriage.

Some young people have violent parents. Having seen that model they may expect partners to be violent. Don't fall into that trap. Healthy couples are not physically violent.

Getting to know you ♥

Ask yourself the following questions to see if either of you is a candidate for a blowup. Is either of you:

- quick to get angry, or does it take a great deal to make you blow?
- a physical communicator? Do you grab people roughly by the arms or pull impatiently when you want attention?

- prone to hitting? Do you get into fights, smack people, or throw things when you're upset?
- known for being a fighter? Have you gotten into trouble with roommates, family, or coworkers for losing your temper?

If you answered yes to any of these questions, seek help. You can learn to control your temper, but don't wait until after you're engaged or married before you start to work on it.

CHAPTER 17

Who Serves Whom?

PATTY SOUNDED *as if she had been released from prison.* "When I was dating Jim he always had the attitude that I was around to make him happy. We couldn't go anywhere or do anything unless he would enjoy it. He would never do anything just because I wanted to. With Steve I get the feeling he is actually looking for things to do that are important to me. He makes me feel like a person."

There is nothing good to be said for self-centeredness. For a partnership to be Christian, it must be established on solid Christian principles. And selfishness is not one of them.

While talking to me about marriage, a friend mentioned a verse. It doesn't use the words *husband, wife, wedding,* or *marriage,* yet it is exactly to the point:

> *Each of you should look not only to your own interests, but also to the interests of others.*
>
> PHILIPPIANS 2:4

The "not only" part suggests I have legitimate interests, needs, expectations. Problems arise when I am so consumed by my own personal needs that I care little for those of my spouse.

One of God's key purposes for creating couples was to make them helpful to each other.

Recognizing self-centeredness

Some of the nicest people you know have become engaged to and married some of the most self-centered, selfish people you know. Did you ask yourself, "How did a nice guy like him fall for such an egotistical twit?" or "Why can't she see what he is really like?" Everyone else saw it.

Any number of factors keep us from seeing reality:

- a limited view of love
- overzealousness to get married
- optimism that a few good qualities outweigh the bad ones
- the fantasy that true love will eventually bring out a loving nature in even the most selfish person
- the belief that a little attention from a selfish person is better than no attention from an unselfish one

Each of us brings our own peculiar ingredients to this problem. The saddest people are those who could have and should have seen the facts but refused to do so.

Part of the reason for our inability to recognize self-centeredness is the overwhelming nature of love. While we are trying to think rationally, an avalanche of emotions is sweeping over us. Who can reason at such a time?

Look for consideration

When Bob and Alicia were dating, he decided it would be a great idea to take her bowling. When he asked, however, she said, "I don't feel like bowling tonight."

Her answer was far from what Bob expected. "What do you mean? Everyone likes to bowl," Bob argued. "If you bowl, you start to feel better automatically."

Alicia disagreed and the two quickly squared off into an ugly battle. Alicia refused to discuss it any further and Bob wasn't about to suggest an alternative.

If Bob could have stepped back and looked at this scene objectively, he might have recognized what he was doing. But he couldn't step back; he was up to his neck in thoughtlessness and selfishness. In fact, he considered himself generous. After all, he was willing to pay Alicia's fee, rent the shoes, and throw in a Goo-Goo bar.

In a calmer moment Bob should have examined his offer.

> *The LORD God said, "It is not good for the man to be alone. I will make a helper suitable for him."*
>
> GENESIS 2:18

He wanted to go bowling and gave Alicia no real choice about it.

When Alicia resisted, Bob demanded.

When Alicia resisted further, Bob became entrenched.

Bob's actions tell us that he was disguising his thoughtlessness in an act of generosity. That doesn't make Bob bad. But it does say he has something to learn before he will make a great husband. He needs to understand and practice being thoughtful.

The real reason

Why do you want to get married? To please someone? Do you want to peel grapes, fetch slippers, and draw bath water?

Probably not.

Most of us are looking instead for others to please us. We want mates who will cook supper, scrape the windshield on frosty mornings, and quote Keats on romantic evenings.

Therein lies the sticky part.

Both parties must receive some benefit from marriage. That's normal and healthy. If one fails to get something out of the union, it will definitely suffer. Each must be paid, even if payment is not totally equal, and problems will arise if one partner gets far more than the other.

Smart couples treat each other with a great deal of loving consideration. Wisdom from above allows us the freedom to do this.

Beware of anyone who sees love as a form of self-

> *Love . . . is not self-seeking.*
>
> 1 CORINTHIANS 13:4–5

gratification. Love asks what it can give, not what it can get.

> *Love is kind.*
>
> 1 CORINTHIANS 13:4

Far from hopeless

Fortunately, selfishness has a high recovery rate if it is treated early and correctly. For many people thoughtlessness is exactly that: something they haven't thought about.

Don't dump a good person because of a handful of selfish habits. Most of us have a pocketful. If you really love each other and are willing to pay the price of improving your relationship, you can do it.

When Jessica met Dave he was barely housebroken. Dave didn't realize he should call if he was going to be late. He thought he was protecting Jessica by never discussing finances. His bachelor days had left him nearly devoid of social skills.

But Jessica loved Dave down to his toes. And she wasn't going to lose him just because he hogged the remote control.

Deliberately and systematically Jessica began pulling the husks off Dave. She told him what she needed to feel loved and secure. She explained how important phone calls were. She reminded him that it was fun to plan activities together.

Dave had never thought about it.

Months later Jessica married a caring guy—Dave—and the two of them still love each other and enjoy learning new ways to meet each other's needs.

Kindness doesn't come naturally. People who have not been the recipients of kindness usually don't know how to show it. But many of them are willing and eager to learn.

Start today

Find out as soon as possible if symptoms of selfishness result from skin-deep thoughtlessness or to-the-core self-centeredness. The cure for the first is a simple cosmetic procedure. The cure for the second involves major surgery.

The test is easy, but you must be open-minded and realistic about the results.

List three things that seem thoughtless to you (for example, he never calls when he's going to be late; she never says thank you; he uses my car and never puts gas in it; she never offers to pay when we go out). You might have problems more severe than these. If so, list the most serious ones.

When you have settled on three, plan your strategy. When, where, and how will you bring up the subject?

Mention one at a time.

Be polite and loving.

Be direct but not rude.

Start by saying something like, "I really enjoy being with you, Sam. But there is something about our relationship that troubles me. Would you mind helping me figure it out?"

Don't be vague, gushy, or excessively apologetic. Appeal to your sweetheart's best instincts. Don't judge your success by the first reaction. He or she may be extremely agreeable but not follow through. On the other hand, he or she may resent your suggestion at first but later change. If you have something great going on, the two of you will survive the confrontation and become even closer and happier.

Confrontation is not evil. Far better to confront in love now than in anger over unresolved issues later.

Look for general success

Love does not conquer all and people do not change simply because we want them to change. If a person cannot or will not improve, you need to know what you are working with.

If there has been progress, be happy because it reveals potential.

This is an excellent time to ask what improvements you can make in yourself. Do not neglect to do this. Your open-

WELL, ENOUGH ABOUT ME. LET'S TALK ABOUT
YOU. WHAT DO YOU THINK OF ME?

ness and willingness to change will encourage the same in a person who loves you.

> *They did not listen or pay attention; they were stiff-necked and would not listen or respond to discipline.*
>
> JEREMIAH 17:23

If there is no change

God was never eager to work with anyone who was stiff-necked and stubborn. Several times He walked away from people for exactly this reason. If you make a few reasonable requests and the only response you get is bristling anger, you might want to follow God's example and walk away. Never marry anyone who is inflexible.

Getting to know you ♥

Evaluate what is happening as you date and plan for the future. Does one of you:

- always get your own way?
- pout when you don't get your way?
- refuse to discuss where to go on dates?
- offer the other person choices but then ignore the suggestions?
- refuse to do things with the other person's family or friends?
- always use close-ended statements (for example, "If I can't have a house with three bedrooms, I'll live in an apartment forever"; "No one has more than two children these days")?

- ask for an opinion and then ignore it?
- buy gifts the other person doesn't want?
- make requests in manipulating terms (for example, "If you really loved me, you would do what I ask")?

If the answer to more than a few of these questions is yes, your problem needs more than cosmetic surgery. Go to an expert for advice.

CHAPTER **18** ♥

Laughing Together

MARTIN AND MARILYN *built their relationship on silliness. They spent most of their dating time poking fun and acting giddy. Like kids at an all-night party, they perceived everything as hilarious. Whether ordering pizza, sitting in a movie theater, or occupying the back pew at church, every activity gave them a reason to chortle, chuckle, and snort. Their common bond was silliness, and they seldom had a serious conversation.*

Larry and Lynn, on the other, hand, were the concrete, practical kind. They discussed purpose and goals on every date. They saw life as a series of building blocks and each was anxious to have a partner who could add to the structure they were building. Not prone to lightness or fun, they were committed to the burdens before them. Their common bond was hard, rock-bottom reality and they concentrated on preparing themselves for the challenges ahead.

Both of these couples stumbled over the same problem. They went to extremes and suffered from lack of balance. Neither knew how to use healthy doses of humor in their relationship. The first couple believed laughter was all that mattered, and the second considered it totally frivolous.

In the reasonable middle roams the couple who knows that partnerships are too important to handle without laughter. They have learned to enjoy the unexpected. Life has so much seriousness that people need to appreciate every amusing turn it takes.

The easiest days to laugh

When describing a person we really like, we almost inevitably say, "He's so funny," or "You'd love her sense of humor."

Humor is one of the common denominators of attraction. No one has ever said to me, "I can't wait for you to meet Sandra; she as dull as an ironing board."

While you are dating you probably laugh easily. You find each other new, refreshing, amusing, even exciting.

People don't marry because they admire a person's lack of personality. The realities of life can change even good-natured people into tyrants if they lack a healthy sense of humor. Bills, illnesses, and communication problems can dry up a sense of humor if it isn't resupplied daily.

I know of no one who has recreated a stodgy partner into an easygoing, light-spirited person after marriage. So if you're dating someone who is humorless, think about what it would be like to live the rest of your life with Cardboard Curt or Grim-Faced Gretchen.

Life's experiences supply enough seriousness. It's up to us to furnish the cheerfulness by finding the good side of living.

> *All the days of the oppressed are wretched, but the cheerful heart has a continual feast.*
>
> PROVERBS 15:15

A reasonable expectation

No one needs to apologize for wanting a happy marriage. It is a reasonable expectation.

Some people differentiate between happiness and joy. Happiness, they say, is the feeling we have when all our circumstances are pleasant. Joy, on the other hand, is having a sense of peace, well-being, and good-nature even when circumstances are unpleasant. Using this definition, we realize that no one can be happy all the time because no one can totally control external circumstances. We can, however, always have joy. And two joyful people inevitably make a great marriage.

We are immature if we run from our responsibilities. We are foolish if we live only for responsibility. Be happy every day you are able. Be joyful. Celebrate life and love every day.

Even the dour, pessimistic author of Ecclesiastes concedes the fact that young people should enjoy happiness when they can find it.

> *B*e happy, young man, while you are young,
> and let your heart give you joy in the days
> of your youth.
>
> ECCLESIASTES 11:9

The joy of life

There is a difference between lightheartedness and lightheadedness. The latter has no clue as to what is important. The former knows that joy is every bit as crucial as seriousness.

Lightheaded folks are unaware of the circumstances. Lighthearted ones say, even when times are tough, "Let's celebrate. We still have this evening to enjoy each other."

I know several couples who have plenty of reasons to complain. One has suffered a series of health problems. Another has been stunned by financial losses. A third couple lives in ongoing grief because of some destructive decisions their daughter has made.

If you were to meet these three couples, you would not be struck by their sadness. Rather you would be impressed by their sense of joy. They have learned to live with loss, yet maintain their appreciation for the gifts of God.

To be near any of them is to benefit from an infectious aura of joy and fulfillment. They have not gotten everything they wanted out of life, but they are enormously thankful for what they have. They don't make speeches about heroics but their countenances say they are indeed heroes.

Compare them to Gloomy Gus and Glenda. They live under a cloud that rains on everyone who gets near them. Life is a burden, a struggle, one sad setback after another. They brighten a room by leaving it.

Couples with the best chance for happiness and satisfaction find joy in simply being alive.

THE WAY YOU CARRY ON YOU'D THINK WE WERE MERE CARTOON CHARACTERS IN A BOOK ON DATING - CHAPTER 18 PAGE 153 TO BE SPECIFIC.

The Bible speaks of joy as an emotion that blooms in adversity. Joy is not the goal of life, but it is an attitude we need if we are to reach our goals.

A joyful person says, "I lost my job, my insurance is due, and my dog threw up on my pillow, but I have so many good things going for me that I know these setbacks are just temporary." When you meet people like that, get to know them right away.

Paul wrote this bit of Christian contrast:

> *Sorrowful, yet always rejoicing; poor, yet making many rich; having nothing, and yet possessing everything*
>
> 2 CORINTHIANS 6:10

We can all count on disappointment. Its arrival is as certain as ragweed in August. What we can't depend on is joy. It doesn't bloom unless it is planted and nurtured.

A gift of the Spirit

If behind your smile you are gritting your teeth and mumbling complaints, you do not have joy. You only have pretense. Joy is not a smile we paste on our faces when the preacher asks how we are when we leave church on Sunday morning. Joy comes from inside. Many people can learn to act joyfully, but only the Holy Spirit can give genuine joy (see Galatians 5:22). That is another reason it is so important to marry someone who shares your Christian faith.

By becoming one with the Spirit our values and our attitudes toward life become more like God's. Those internal changes help us appreciate life for what it actually has to offer. As a result, our reason for living goes beyond the present and the finite. We see a bigger picture. We know that today's circumstances and how we react to them have future and eternal significance.

Janet spoke of joy but only with her words. She knew the Bible said she should have joy so she insisted she had it. Her actions, however, contradicted her words. Her behavior was vengeful, cross, and mean-spirited. If her husband teased her for being grumpy or tried to help her see a brighter side of a situation, she snapped back like a stretched rubber band. But the next Sunday she would stand up in her Sunday school class and tell how she had maintained joy when others were persecuting her.

People who have joy act joyfully. They possess a contagious sense of well-being.

If the two of you lack joy in your relationship, make sure you both know the source of all joy. If you do, practice looking at your circumstances from God's perspective, keeping His eternal values in mind, and you will realize that temporary inconvenience, discomfort, or unpleasantness have no eternal significance. When we learn to see beyond circumstances, we find joy.

Cutting humor

The kind of humor that puts down the people we love is highly dangerous. Making fun of how someone looks, how he talks, or what she believes can cut deeply and injure the relationship. If there is something we don't like about our friend's humor, it's best to discuss it early and establish a few ground rules:

> Don't make jokes about my mother.
>
> Jokes about my cooking upset me.
>
> I'm very sensitive about being bald.
>
> Don't make fun of my intelligence.
>
> It's okay to kid me about some things, but don't keep bringing it up.
>
> I don't like weight jokes.
>
> I can't help it if I don't read very fast.

People who love each other need to back off when they discover that their sense of humor is hurtful. That is especially true if their humor is heavy on the put-down side. Damaging humor should never be part of a loving relationship.

On the other hand, we do not want to be too touchy about what is said. Sometimes we need to laugh at ourselves, especially if the jokes are light and good-natured.

Getting to know you ♥

1. Do the two of you lean too much toward either silliness or seriousness? What can you do to become more balanced?

2. Did either of you come from a family that was unbalanced in this area? Discuss how the patterns you learned at home affect your relationship.

3. Do you ever get into trouble or offend people because of your sense of humor? Discuss how this could affect your future.

4. Do people stay away from you because the two of you are never any fun? Discuss how this could affect your future.

CHAPTER **19** ♥

Respect for Time and Space

WHEN MY WIFE, PAT, and I travel together to speak at seminars, we often spend a week or two in cramped quarters. We sleep in motel rooms, cabins, and dormitories. And we travel in a compact car, so sometimes we drive for ten hours never more than a few inches from each other.

There are many advantages to living like sardines. But there are also a number of disadvantages: We grow tired of one another. Our politeness wears thin. Our conversation becomes boring. Our idiosyncrasies become annoying.

These jaunts across the country have taught us the need for individual time and space. There is nothing wrong with us or with our affection. But we do sometimes become tired of each other's presence.

Our need for "space" when traveling led us to discover the therapeutic value of parks, shopping malls, and grocery stores. We park the car in some gigantic lot and say, "Meet you at the ice cream store in two hours."

We don't separate because our relationship has fallen apart. Rather we pull apart to keep it together.

> *Jesus was praying in private.*
>
> LUKE 9:18

Christ apparently enjoyed being with people. Scripture shows Him interacting with big crowds, small groups, and individuals—whatever the situation called for. He attended weddings, parties, and feasts.

But at other times He wanted and needed solitude. On several occasions He quietly disappeared to be alone.

Jesus looked for opportunities to be alone with God. He didn't want or need the disciples trailing behind Him every moment.

Time to ponder

When the shepherds came to see the Christ child, they created a tremendous commotion, spreading the word that the Savior had come.

How did Mary feel at that moment? It will always be a mystery because the Bible only says:

> *Mary treasured up all these things and pondered them in her heart.*
>
> LUKE 2:19

Each of us has thoughts, memories, and desires stored up in our hearts that we ponder from time to time. Some are bright and enjoyable. Others are dark and mysterious even to ourselves. We are entitled to ponder these mysteries. No law of relationship demands that we reveal every thought of passion we have ever entertained.

The idea is disclosure—especially to the person you love. But timing is critical and no one should demand to know how a partner feels about everything every moment.

People who are in love want to know as much as possible about each other, so asking questions is a perfectly natural and healthy activity. But learn to be tactful and loving in the way you ask. A gardener can have carefully pruned vines or ones that have been cut back so far they will never grow again.

My wife keeps a set of notes in her Bible. I think they are prayer requests or subjects she wants to meditate on, but I'm not positive. I've never read them. I wouldn't think of it. When Pat wants me to know what she's grappling with, she will tell me. I want to know what she wants me to know when she wants me to know it. Every bit and nothing more. Then and not before.

To live where no thought is private, no dream is personal, would be too much transparency.

The gift of privacy

Pat and I have no secrets from each other but we respect each other's privacy. Be cautious of the person who says, "There will be no secrets between me and my spouse." The real meaning of this statement may be that there will be no privacy. No privacy means there is no place to weigh values or to contemplate ideas. What a miserable marriage it would be if each partner were expected to reveal, explain, and defend every new thought or idea.

Having secrets is different from having privacy. A secret is information I need to know that is being withheld from me. Secrets shouldn't exist in an intimate relationship.

The newspaper tells of a man who was arrested for income tax evasion. His young bride said they had been married only a short time and she knew nothing about his business. Apparently in a hurry to marry, she didn't ask many

I NEED SOME TIME TO GET AWAY
BY MYSELF AND THINK. WILL YOU COME
WITH ME?

questions and he didn't tell her much about himself. That's too much secrecy. She had every right to know more about him. He had information she needed to know.

But what of the woman who has always wondered what happened to the man she used to date? Or the man who feels he failed by dropping out of college? What of the wife who feels guilty because she moved far away from her mother? Should a spouse get out an emotional crowbar to pry out every last thought about such matters? I think not.

The role of a loving spouse is not to find out every private thought; it is to create an accepting atmosphere in which a mate will feel free to share when the time and circumstances are right.

One of the most frightening prospects of marriage is the fear of total intimacy. No roommate, no brother or sister, no parent has known you as well as a spouse will. That's scary. Most of us are not sure we want to be known that thoroughly.

The good news is that none of us has to reveal every feeling, every thought, and every apprehension we have. Each of us has corners we are not ready to show anyone.

That's all right. Good partners allow each other the time and space they need. And they are ready to listen when the other wants to talk.

The gift of silence

The tongue is a voluntary muscle. It does not run automatically and need not run incessantly. God has given us the option of resting our vocal cords and idling our jaws for hours at a time.

While we acknowledge the value of communication, we also accept the importance of silence. With televisions, radios, and compact discs blaring, we have come to look at silence as somehow deviant and harmful.

The Bible reminds us, however, that there is a time for both. Beware of a partner who never allows you to talk. Be just as leery of someone who demands that you talk all the time.

> *There is . . . a time to be silent and a time to speak.*
>
> ECCLESIASTES 3:1, 7

Educate each other about the strength born in silence. Some well-meaning people distrust silence. They fear that if their companions aren't talking, they are unhappy. They take silence as a personal affront, as if it means their partners are unhappy in their company or are irritated about something.

Silence is terribly hard to interpret. It can take months or years for a person to decipher what silence means in another. Speed up the process by explaining your quiet moments.

What does silence mean to you? Are you quiet because you are content? Afraid? Weighing difficult decisions? Planning your future? Upset?

You might also help by learning to control your silence. The verse from Ecclesiastes also says there is a time to talk. Silence can be used as a way of gaining control over someone. Talking is not the only way to dominate a conversation. We also manage communication by refusing to participate. Then, in self-righteousness, we reason, "How could I wreck the communication if I didn't say anything?"

Precisely.

Respect for silence cuts both ways: (1) We must accept a person's right and need for silence; (2) We must recognize the potential damage silence can create.

Since people all come from different backgrounds and have different personalities, everyone views speaking and silence differently. One family talked all through dinner and the other treated meals as time for monastic contemplation. When we marry we tend to expect our new relationships to be similar to the ones we are used to. That's unfair. We are unreasonable to expect spouses to fit the patterns of our pasts.

A more sensible approach is for a couple to develop their own form of communication, each learning to respect the other's times of silence and speech.

Getting to know you ♥

1. Does either of you sometimes feel smothered by the other's presence? Discuss ways to relieve this problem.

2. On a scale of 1 (enjoy) to 10 (abhor), how do you feel about spending time apart? What agreement can you reach about how much independence you each need?

3. Does either of you think the other has too many secrets? How can you resolve this if it's a problem?

4. Does one of you do most of the talking? What would encourage the quiet one to talk more?

CHAPTER 20

Faithful and Committed

WE LIVE IN THE GELATIN GENERATION. Things that used to be solid are quivering masses. Things we want to depend on are frequently unstable and unreliable.

Marriage, for many, has become one of those uncertain experiences. But it doesn't have to be. Couples can enter a relationship with determined commitment. Instead of asking if the marriage will work they can concentrate on how to make it work.

Never take commitment for granted

If you expect commitment in marriage, make sure you both share that value. When one of you thinks marriage is for a lifetime and the other thinks it lasts only as long as it's fun, chances are it won't be fun for long. And just because both of you are Christians doesn't guarantee that you agree in this area. The best way to know for sure is to discuss your definition of commitment.

The difficulty with youth

Teenagers seldom are ready to settle down. Unsure of what they want in the future and uncertain about who they really are, they make some serious mistakes in choosing mates. Although they mean well and have good intentions, they make promises they are unable to keep.

Expecting teenagers to make lifelong commitments stretches their capacities. The characteristics of youth are spontaneity, curiosity, even restlessness. These make miserable qualities in marriage.

The double package

Love without *faithfulness* is a contradiction in terms. To express love in one sentence and admit unfaithfulness in the next is like saying the house is built well but the foundation is made of cardboard. It may look good but there is nothing substantial holding it up.

God's promise to us is a double package:

> *Love and faithfulness meet together;*
> *righteousness and peace kiss each other.*
>
> PSALM 85:10

Imagine God saying, "I love you; I love you not . . . ." Today He loves us, tomorrow He writes us out of His will. One minute He promises to be with us always, the next day He announces that He is only available on Thursday afternoons.

> *Let your "Yes" be "Yes," and your "No," "No"; anything beyond this comes from the evil one.*
>
> MATTHEW 5:37

If there is a lack of faithfulness and you are afraid to talk about it, you are inviting big-time trouble.

If either of you is fickle or unfaithful, the good news is that people change. No gauge has yet been devised to measure the degree of commitment a person will have ten years from today. The less faithful one may become as dependable as the swallows that return every year to San Juan Capistrano, while the solidly committed one may degenerate into a slippery lizard.

Nevertheless, it's best to start with a dependable person. To marry a fickle person and hope for a miracle is to play the fool.

What are your words worth?

When Brian made a promise, he never intended to keep it. He would give his word and then start looking for ways to get out of it. Brian never considered his word binding. If he promised to pay a debt on Thursday, he would ask himself, "What can they do if I don't pay it?" He used more energy trying to get out of

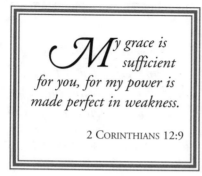

My grace is sufficient for you, for my power is made perfect in weakness.

2 CORINTHIANS 12:9

promises than he did trying to keep them.

If Brian's word was so worthless you might think he would soon be friendless. Quite the contrary. He was so charming and winsome that people overlooked his obvious character flaw. "That's Brian," they would say with a smile after hearing another story about his irresponsible exploits.

Marriage partners can't afford to be that generous. If someone's word is worthless, the person will make a pitiful partner no matter what other endearing qualities might be vying for recognition.

Although faithfulness seems to be a reasonable expectation for a marriage partner, people frequently marry those whose word is an empty bubble.

When asked about her husband's habit of chasing other women, Joan replied that she wasn't worried because she would be by his side to fight off intruders. Seeing her husband as a weak, innocent victim of loose, over powering women, she appointed herself his moral bodyguard. She didn't expect him to keep his word because that would be impossible for anyone as morally feeble as he.

If you believe that no one is strong enough to remain morally pure, you are devaluing yourself, others, and God.

Christ was concerned about people who made promises and then looked for clever ways to get out of them. They argue, "Well, yes, I promised but . . . ." They then make excuses for not keeping their word. Jesus Christ told us to be simple, sincere, and direct.

Some refuse to understand open, honest commitment. Eventually they hurt everyone around them.

A sense of loyalty

A sales associate for a small Dodge dealership went looking for a new car for his own family—and bought a Chevrolet.

When he arrived at work Monday his boss was waiting for him. She handed the man a severance check and a plastic bag with all of his personal belongings. There was no discussion. The sales manager knew that customers would not understand why her sales associate drove a Chevy.

Loyalty is paramount. In marriage loyalty is the core of unity.

The apostle Paul felt comfortable with a handful of Christians because he had seen their loyalty. He didn't have to start each day by asking, "Well, are you with me or against me today?" Their behavior, both in his presence and away from him, was consistent.

No couple should live in doubt. The commitment of each should be total and beyond suspicion.

> *I ask you, loyal yokefellow, help those women who have contended at my side in the cause of the gospel, along with Clement and the rest of my fellow workers, whose names are in the book of life.*
>
> PHILIPPIANS 4:3

Let no one separate

God did not intend that any married couple should separate. His plan from the beginning was that marriage should last a lifetime. Look squarely at what Jesus Christ said:

> *S*o they are no longer two, but one. Therefore what God has joined together, let man not separate.
>
> MATTHEW 19:6

Every marriage should begin with that same promise. Marriage is for a lifetime.

An honest conversation about the permanence of marriage should take place before a ring ever slides onto a finger.

...FROM THIS DAY FORWARD TIL "FUN" DO US PART.

No one can predict the future, but it's wise to begin your union in total agreement about the durability of marriage.

Is either of you a product of the Let's Try It school of matrimony? Does one of you consider career or geography or recreation or education more important than a lasting marriage?

Too often I hear stories like this:

One partner receives a promotion that requires relocation. The spouse is unwilling to make that move. After two weeks of heated discussion, one leaves to start a new job; the other remains behind. A few months later the one who stayed files for divorce.

Executives, blue-collar workers teachers, ministers— this story is repeated about couples from all walks of life. If either of you is too job-centered or location-centered that you won't move to keep your marriage intact, now is the time to find out.

The marriage vows most of us make say:

For richer, for poorer;
In sickness and in health,
Till death parts us.

This is a promise two people make to each other before God and other witnesses. There is nothing conditional about it.

Getting to know you ♥

Discuss the following: Is it okay to

- make promises and not keep them?
- switch plans without warning or explanation?
- try marriage to see if it works?

- bounce from one serious relationship to another?
- be secretive and mysterious?

If there were only one recipe for lasting relationships, we would all get bored with the menu. But there are many recipes, and there is nothing boring about romance and marriage.

Before you look to your jeweler for an engagement ring, look to Christ for wisdom and direction.

Note to the Reader

The publisher invites you to share your response to the message of this book by writing Discovery House Publishers, Box 3566, Grand Rapids, MI 49501, USA. For information about other Discovery House books, music, or videos, contact us at the same address or call 1-800-653-8333. Find us on the Internet at http://www.dhp.org/ or send e-mail to books@dhp.org.